The Black Ar

HORROR OF
FANG ROCK

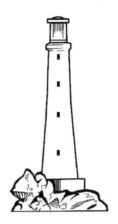

By Matthew Guerrieri

Published July 2019 by Obverse Books

Cover Design © Cody Schell

Text © Matthew Guerrieri, 2019

Range Editors: Philip Purser-Hallard, Paul Simpson

Matthew would like to thank:

Ethan Iverson and Jack Miller, for taking the time to read and comment on early drafts; Philip Purser-Hallard and Paul Simpson for their expertise and editing judgement; and Lucy and Helena, for their love, support, and understanding.

For Lucy,

eine Sonne mir in schwerer Nacht

'And so this tower cutting through
the breadth and depth of heaven beacons to the farthest
distances
by day, and all night long the sailors borne on the waves
will see the great flame blazing from its top –
nor miss his aim: though he run to the Bull's Horn,
he'll find Zeus the Saviour, sailing, Proteus, by this beam.'

[Posidippus, epigram for the dedication of the Pharos at
Alexandria (third century BCE), trans Frank Nisetich]

'I died at sea.
Quickly (he was in a hurry himself, a traveller in a foreign
land)
Leophantus bewailed and buried me.
But I am too small to thank Leophantus in a large way.'

[Posidippus, epigram for the victim of a shipwreck (third
century BCE), trans Frank Nisetich][1]

---

[1] Posidippus, *The New Posidippus: A Hellenistic Poetry Book*, pp42,
38.

Also available

CONTENTS

OVERVIEW

Serial Title: *Horror of Fang Rock*

Writer: Terrance Dicks

Director: Paddy Russell

Original UK Transmission Dates: 3 September 1977 – 24 September 1977

Running Time: Episode 1: 24m 12s

Episode 2: 24m 10s

Episode 3: 23m 14s

Episode 4: 23m 48s

UK Viewing Figures: Episode 1: 6.8 million

Episode 2: 7.1 million

Episode 3: 9.8 million

Episode 4: 9.9 million

Regular Cast: Tom Baker (Doctor Who), Louise Jameson (Leela)

Guest Cast: Colin Douglas (Reuben), John Abbott (Vince), Ralph Watson (Ben), Sean Caffrey (Lord Palmerdale), Alan Rowe (Skinsale), Rio Fanning (Harker), Annette Woollett (Adelaide)

Antagonists: Rutan scout

Novelisation: *Doctor Who and the Horror of Fang Rock* by Terrance Dicks. **The Target Doctor Who Library** #32.

Responses:

'[T]he Elgin Marbles of Base-Under-Siege stories [...] it's a claustrophobic, beautiful-looking period drama in which everyone dies; what's not to like?'

[Joe Briggs-Ritchie, 'The Ballad of Fang Rock,' *The Doctor Who Ratings Guide*, 8 May 2010]

'The pace is painfully slow, the characterisation is wooden, and the dialogue is made of baked beans. Nevertheless, there is a special kind of pleasure to be derived from sitting at home and watching one actor being paid to say to another actor things like "Have you taken leave of your senses?"'

[Richard Boston, 'Enough to Drive a Man to Drink'. *The Observer*, 25 September 1977, p27]

SYNOPSIS

Episode 1

A glowing object falls from the sky into the sea near the remote Fang Rock lighthouse, observed only by a young lighthouse-keeper, **Vince**. His older colleague **Reuben** and their supervisor **Ben** dismiss his observation, even when an unexpected night fog rises around the rocky island and their electric generator – a new technology of which Reuben is suspicious – begins to fail intermittently. Ben dies, apparently electrocuted while repairing the ground-floor generator, and his body is found by **the Doctor**, who has been attempting to take **Leela** to Brighton. Vince trusts the newcomers, but Reuben fears that they are foreign spies. Rather than use the lighthouse's telegraph to apprise the mainland of Ben's death, he promises to use semaphore in daylight.

Leela goes outside to hunt for the electricity-manipulating alien who the Doctor is convinced has actually killed Ben. Meanwhile Vince finds his friend's body gone, and responds with superstitious terror. From the lamp-gallery, the Doctor and Reuben spot a steam-yacht foundering offshore. With the light out of action, and despite the lighthouse crew's best attempts to warn the yacht with siren and flares, the boat is wrecked on Fang Rock.

Episode 2

The Doctor, Reuben and Vince have rescued some survivors from the yacht: the millionaire financier **Lord Palmerdale**; his friend **Skinsale**, an army colonel turned MP; and Palmerdale's secretary **Adelaide**. Left to tend the siren, Leela has seen a luminous tentacled shape moving across the rocks beneath the lighthouse.

8

Reuben believes that she has seen 'the Beast of Fang Rock', a legendary sea-creature supposedly involved in an incident in the 1820s in which two keepers died and the third went mad. A fourth survivor of the yacht, the coxswain **Harker**, finds Ben's mutilated body in the water. The Doctor believes that the creature has performed a post-mortem to learn about human anatomy.

It transpires that Palmerdale's party were en route from Deauville, where Skinsale had given the financier illicit inside trading information to pay off his gambling debts, to London via a private train from Southampton. Skinsale is bitter about his moral failure, and Palmerdale is desperate to get to the mainland so he can use the information to make a fortune on the stock market. He tries to bribe Harker to telegraph his brokers, but the coxswain attacks him in revenge for the sailors who died in the wreck. The Doctor interrupts them, explaining that the creature is planning an attack on the lighthouse. Stoking the generator's boiler beneath them, Reuben steps outside and is attacked.

Episode 3

The Doctor and Leela go out to look for Reuben, but he returns, subdued and apparently traumatised, and locks himself in the crew's sleeping-quarters, where he stands eerily glowing. Skinsale overhears Palmerdale bribing Vince to send his coded message, and after distracting Adelaide he sabotages the telegraph to preserve his own reputation. To avoid the Doctor discovering his duplicity Palmerdale hides outside the lamp-room on the lamp gallery, and is attacked by the creature, which has climbed up the outside of the lighthouse. Vince burns the money and the message Palmerdale gave him. The Doctor, Harker and Skinsale find

Palmerdale's body outside, and learn that he was electrocuted before he fell.

In the boiler room, Harker is surprised by the arrival of Reuben, who kills him in the same way as the others. After finding Harker's body, the Doctor and Leela stumble upon Reuben's, and realise that he has been dead for hours. The Doctor deduces that the alien is a shapeshifter, and is locked inside the lighthouse with them.

Episode 4

The false Reuben seeks out Vince in the lamp-room and electrocutes him. The Doctor finds the power relay that has been draining the generator, and realises that the stranded alien is diverting the energy to a distress beacon. He finds a signal modulator in the crew quarters, but is forced to hide from 'Reuben' by dangling out of the window. Meanwhile 'Reuben' kills Adelaide. The Doctor sends Leela and Skinsale up to the lamp room while he keeps the alien talking. It reverts to its natural form and the Doctor identifies it as a **Rutan**. A military scout, it has identified Earth as a potential strategic stronghold in its people's war with the Sontarans, who will inevitably destroy the planet in retaliation. It is killing the humans on the island to keep its presence secret while it signals to its mothership.

The Doctor, Leela and Skinsale temporarily discourage the Rutan with gunpowder from the maroon flares, and the Doctor plans to modify the carbon-arc lantern to generate a beam powerful enough to destroy the mothership. A vital component is a large diamond. Skinsale searches Palmerdale's corpse and finds a bag of diamonds. The Doctor selects one and discards the rest. Distracted by trying to retrieve them, Skinsale is killed by the returning Rutan, leaving only the Doctor and Leela alive. Leela kills the Rutan with a flare-launcher and the Doctor destroys the approaching mothership. The explosion temporarily blinds Leela, and permanently changes the colour of her eyes. As they leave, the Doctor quotes 'The Ballad of Flannan Isle' by Wilfred Gibson.

PROLOGUE

PALMERDALE

Are you in charge here?

DOCTOR

No, but I'm full of ideas.

[*Horror of Fang Rock* episode 2[2]]

On Sunday, November 22, 1987, at 11.00pm, WTTW-TV, Chicago's main Public Broadcasting System affiliate, began airing its weekly rerun of **Doctor Who**. That night's instalment was just over a decade old: *Horror of Fang Rock*, first transmitted by the BBC in September of 1977. It is one of the series' most effectively claustrophobic stories, a web of invasion, suspicion, and death, set in and around the cramped confines of a most unusual fortress: a lighthouse.

In Chicago, Illinois, the skyscrapers are, by necessity, inland lighthouses. Chicago long had lighthouses of the more usual sort – ever since 1832, when one Samuel Jackson built a 40-foot-tall beacon at the juncture of the Chicago River and Lake Michigan (Jackson's second try; the first, ignominiously, collapsed shortly before completion) – but, once the city grew upward, so did its obstacles, and so did its warning lights. Boats and aircraft both have their blinking towers.

The skyscrapers also flash invisible light: radio waves, television

---

[2] This and all quotations from the story throughout come from the episodes as broadcast.

broadcasts, cellular transmissions, signals across the electromagnetic spectrum. In 1987, the broadcast signal of WTTW, converted into a narrow beam of microwaves, would travel eight miles from the station's studios, on the city's northwest side, to an antenna on top of the Sears Tower – for a time, the tallest building in the world, a useful vantage for line-of-sight transmission. From there the signal fanned out across the greater Chicagoland area, as far north as southern Wisconsin, as far west as the southeast corner of Michigan. Such signals, it turns out, are unexpectedly vulnerable. All you need is a bright enough beacon, in electrical terms: point a stronger beam of microwaves at the antenna, and it will instead send **that** signal out to millions of televisions. Which is apparently how, on that November evening, WTTW's broadcast of *Horror of Fang Rock* was interrupted for a minute and 23 seconds by a barely-intelligible video of a guy in a Max Headroom mask.

It wasn't the first instance of a broadcast signal intrusion. The year before, John MacDougall, moonlighting at a satellite telecommunications port in Florida, had hijacked the signal feed of HBO, replacing it with a text message complaining about the channel's service fees. In September of 1987, viewers of the Playboy Channel were briefly confronted with a biblical message encouraging their repentance. (Another television engineer, Thomas Haynie – an employee of the Christian Broadcasting Network – was the culprit.) But the 'Max Headroom incident' became the touchstone for broadcast hijacking, partly because the perpetrators were never caught, partly because it was so strange[3].

---

[3] For a comprehensive account of the Max Headroom incident, see Knittel, Chris, 'The Mystery of the Creepiest Television Hack',

Even now, footage of the incident (readily available on that murkiest of modern searchlights, the internet[4]) seems to come from some liminal zone, an inside joke so far inside – and, at the same time, so widely spread – as to instil hermetic disquiet. The frame of the joke, at least, was easily recognisable: Max Headroom, the supposedly computer-generated talking head (normally played, in heavy makeup, by actor Matt Frewer) who first appeared in a dystopian, 1985 made-for-TV science-fiction film broadcast on Great Britain's Channel 4, then became the host of a British music-video programme, then crossed the Atlantic for an eponymous dramatic series on the ABC network[5].

But the WTTW intruder was far less polished, and far more esoteric. The ersatz Max Headroom prattled away in an obscured, distorted voice as a sheet of corrugated metal spun in the background (a low-tech simulation of the 1980s computer graphics pervading the original Headroom's cyberspace habitat). He derided Chicago sportscaster Chuck Swirsky as a 'fricking liberal'. He riffed on the 1980s American cola wars, brandishing a Pepsi can while blurting out Coca-Cola's 'Catch the Wave' slogan. He brandished a prosthetically-augmented middle finger. He dropped in a drive-by reference to the 1959-60 animated series **Clutch Cargo**. And then, after an abrupt cut, one saw the counterfeit Max, on all fours, his

---

[4] For example, 'Max Headroom WTTW Pirating Incident – 11/22/87 Subtitled'.

[5] *Max Headroom: 20 Minutes into the Future*, directed by Rocky Morton and Annabel Jankel, premiered on Channel 4 on April 4, 1985. **The Max Headroom Show** ran on Channel 4 from April 1985 until March 1987. **Max Headroom** aired on the ABC network between March 1987 and May 1988.

pants down, as a woman in a French maid costume slapped his buttocks with a flyswatter.

One could, if one wanted, posit a rational explanation. A couple hours before the WTTW takeover, the same pranksters had briefly cut into the television signal of WGN-TV, one of Chicago's local media powerhouses. WGN's engineering was more watertight: the audio of the intruding broadcast was buried under an oppressive buzz, and the pirate transmission was swiftly switched out. (WGN's sports anchor Dan Roan, then on the air, responded with composed bewilderment: 'If you're wondering what happened,' he said, 'so am I.') On WTTW, the hijacker still had WGN on his mind. Swirsky was, at the time, a WGN employee. Other disparaging references to WGN and its owner, the *Chicago Tribune*, suggested a grudge. The prank could have been the work of that perennial capitalist apostate, a disgruntled employee[6].

But the broadcast's sheer, unmotivated weirdness upstaged such prosaic possibilities. A written description renders the incident more coherent and comprehensible than it really was. It was a drive-by burst of disconnected, subconscious fury, a sudden half-memory of a frantic dream. Thousands of viewers absorbed (or not) in the antics of a time-travelling eccentric abruptly became witnesses to a seeming slippage in reality.

I was one of them, parked in front of the television in the basement of a suburban house northwest of Chicago. And what I remember most about the incident was its very particular disorientation: an obvious interruption, but one congruous enough with the

---

[6] Knittel, 'The Mystery of the Creepiest Television Hack'.

atmosphere of *Horror of Fang Rock* that, for a few seconds, distinctions of context seemed to completely dissolve.

Intrusion and discontinuity provoke and inform *Horror of Fang Rock*. The three men manning the Fang Rock lighthouse at the turn of the 20th century see their routine interrupted by three visiting parties. First, a Rutan scout – a lethal , shapeshifting alien able to take on the appearance of its victims – reconnoitring Earth as a possible redoubt for a Rutan force in galaxy-wide conflict with their long-time enemies, the Sontarans. Then the Doctor, a Time Lord from the planet Gallifrey, roving the universe in a rickety TARDIS with Leela, his warrior companion, aiming for a seaside holiday but diverted to a less hospitable shore. And finally, Lord Palmerdale, a nouveau riche speculator rushing back to England, his secretary Adelaide, and Skinsale, a politician who has given Palmerdale inside information; their yacht runs aground in the fog, leaving the trio and Harker, the yacht's pilot, soaked and stranded. The light flickers and repeatedly fails. The Rutan begins to kill off the assembled humans, one by one, as it summons a Rutan mother ship to claim Earth from its expendable human population. The Doctor races to determine the nature of the threat before it is too late.

Horror of Fang Rock represents **Doctor Who** at a peak. The show and its protagonist had come a long way from its 1963 premiere. Tom Baker brought the series to new heights of popularity: the just-ended 14th season had generated the show's best-ever average viewership[7]. *Fang Rock*'s writer, Terrance Dicks, was

---

[7] In 1976, **Doctor Who** averaged 10.69 million viewers per episode, a mark not surpassed until 2009. See 'Statistics', *Doctor Who Guide*.

unusually fluent in **Doctor Who**, having been associated with the show for nearly a decade, and having written two previous scripts featuring Baker's Doctor.

But *Fang Rock* also found **Doctor Who** in transition. Producer Philip Hinchcliffe and script editor Robert Holmes had infused **Who** with darker elements of horror and violence, drawing viewers but also the ire of the tenacious, reactionary Mary Whitehouse and her National Viewers' and Listeners' Association. Hinchcliffe was replaced by Graham Williams after season 14; Holmes would leave soon after *Fang Rock*. Even filming was on unfamiliar ground: a lack of available London studio space shifted production to the BBC's Pebble Mill studios in Birmingham. Baker, unhappy with the changes, was moody and difficult, creating tension palpable in the end product.

The circumstances – a well-tuned machine suddenly thrown into a different gear – somehow engendered a classic. *Horror of Fang Rock* is lean, taut, effective. The change of studio created more concise visual and spatial styles, realised by a more eager technical crew. (Director Paddy Russell recalled that, back in London, **Doctor Who** was 'a chore, it was bitty, it had gone on a long time and nobody loved it. But up there, it was new.'[8]) Dicks' script is one of the most efficient **Who** would ever enjoy. Even Baker's surliness worked to the story's advantage, putting everyone around him appropriately on edge.

An isolated Edwardian lighthouse; mysterious deaths; an unexpected shipwreck; a body-snatching alien. *Fang Rock* is usually

---

[8] 'Production', *In-Vision* #24, p4.

considered a holdover, a late dose of Holmes' and Hinchcliffe's gothic horror[9]. But it is also, perhaps, the series' most focussed and pointed exploitation of its particular habitat: the blurry boundary between science fiction and horror, between the terror of the unknown and the terror of knowing, between determination of **how** and the often-indeterminable **why**. The WTTW signal hijacker inadvertently chose an appropriate frame for his broadside. *Fang Rock*, too, features unwanted, eerily-disguised presences (the extraterrestrial Rutan), irreverent interventions (by the Doctor himself), and, of course, interrupted beacons.

Story and setting thus form an unusual symbiosis. Like a lighthouse, the story both reflects and projects the centuries of literary and dramatic mythos surrounding lighthouses. In fact, what gives *Fang Rock* its unusual resonance within **Doctor Who**'s larger narrative is how the quirky and contradictory symbolism surrounding lighthouses parallels the quirky and contradictory qualities of that equally singular character, the Doctor. Like the Doctor, a lighthouse is both a beacon of knowledge and wisdom and an indicator of danger. Like the Doctor, a lighthouse is in human society and civilisation, but also apart from it. And like the Doctor, lighthouses seem to attract unusual goings-on, unexpected invasions, dark mysteries. For once, the usual incongruity of the Doctor's presence is muted by the consonance between him and the setting. The Doctor is a strange figure; lighthouses are strange places.

History doesn't so much weigh on *Horror of Fang Rock* as swirl

---

[9] *Fang Rock* was not the only such remainder; *Image of the Fendahl* (1977), for instance, commissioned by Holmes, followed later in the season and recreates a similar atmosphere.

through it, permeate it, like a mist – the history of lighthouses, of their construction, of their operation, of their adoption as metaphor. Can a beam through that fog reveal something about *Fang Rock*? On that WTTW broadcast, the fake Max Headroom interrupted the first scene between Leela and Vince, the youngest member of the lighthouse crew. Vince tells Leela that he assuages the loneliness of the job by heading out to the rocks and talking to the seals. 'That is stupid,' she scolds. 'You should talk often with the old ones of the tribe. That is the only way to learn.'[10] Vince, chastened, offers to get his guest a hot drink, at which point the picture stuttered, the horizontal and vertical hold began to slip, and a different sort of stranger appeared, a disguised invader, riding a stream of (microwave) light, opening up a crack in the narrative.

It's in such cracks that the real texture of the episode resides, in the technology of lighthouses, in the hints and assumptions of the society around them, in the fictional and historical overtones that echo through them. So, it is into such cracks that we will venture. A jury of *Fang Rock*'s artistic peers – authors and scholars, novels and inventions, poems and an opera – will interrogate the tale, its sharp divisions of class and belief, its competing narratives of technological progress and teleological purpose. Historical forces (and coincidences) will testify to the story's uneasy gap between expertise and explanation.

Look, there's a fog coming up. Adjust the lamp; pour something hot. Maybe the old ones can teach us something.

---

[10] *Horror of Fang Rock* episode 1.

PART 1: TECHNOLOGY AND CHARACTER

'Even the mechanical engineer comes at last to an end of his figures, and must stand up, a practical man, face to face with the discrepancies of nature and the hiatuses of theory.'

[Robert Louis Stevenson, 'Records of a Family of Engineers'][11]

1.

Robert Louis Stevenson did not live to see the lighthouse his cousin built on the Flannan Isles. In 1894, the writer suffered a cerebral haemorrhage at his villa on the Samoan island of Upolo. He was 44. The Samoans, bereft, buried him on the mountain overlooking his home. It is called Mount Vaea, named after the mythical Samoan hero who married Apa'ula, from neighbouring, hostile Fiji. As the story goes, when Apa'ula returned to Fiji to give birth to their child, Vaea so fixed his expectant gaze on the ocean's horizon that he began to turn to stone. By the time his wife returned, in grief – her vengeful brothers killed the child – Vaea could only move enough to mouth the words ''Ua sau Apa'ula, ua tautua': 'Apa'ula is here, but too late'[12].

Lighthouses were the Stevenson family business. Thomas Smith established the connection, parlaying an expertise in lamps and reflectors into a job as First Engineer to the Northern Lighthouse

---

[11] Stevenson, Robert Louis, 'Records of a Family of Engineers', in Covin, Sidney, ed, *Letters and Miscellanies of Robert Louis Stevenson* vol XVIII, p261.

[12] See Schultz, E, 'The Samoan Version of the Story of Apakura', *The Journal of the Polynesian Society*, vol XVIII, no 70, June 1909.

Trust, formed in 1786 to build beacons marking the dangerous shoals and rocks surrounding Scotland. But it was Smith's stepson, Robert Stevenson, Robert Louis Stevenson's grandfather and namesake, who anchored the dynasty with a series of daring constructions. Most audacious was the Bell Rock lighthouse, a tower perched on a stone berg that, for all but a few hours each day, lurked a few feet under the North Sea's surface, lying in lethal wait for ships. For three years, Robert Stevenson and a small crew worked during low tide before retreating to a temporary barracks, perched on stilts, to wait out the sea. Finished in 1810, the 35-meter tower was, at the time, the tallest offshore lighthouse in the world, a miracle of engineering. Robert Stevenson's fame and career were assured.

Three of Robert's sons – Alan, David, and Thomas – followed their father into the lighthouse trade. Thomas's son was a sickly child, a late reader and indifferent student who nevertheless began inventing his own tales at an early age. Still, the expectation was that Robert Louis Stevenson would pursue the family calling, and, at the age of 17, he dutifully took up engineering studies at the University of Edinburgh. In the summers, he joined his father as he supervised the construction of various Stevenson-designed outposts around the Scottish coast. His most vivid memories surrounded the building of a light on Dhu Heartach, 'The Black Rock', which, along with the nearby Torran Rocks, had long endangered ships. The feat rivalled the Bell Rock in its degree of difficulty. Granite stones quarried on the island of Erraid were ferried 14 miles southwest, across open seas, winched up the sheer rock, and dovetailed into place. Robert, however, observed the process with a writer's eye, not an engineer's. At one point, one of the building crew fell off a ladder and was ferried back for medical attention. Stevenson sailed to a nearby island in search of a doctor, where he was greeted by a contingent of the crew's wives and children:

> 'It would have been a strange study for any student of human nature to see how quietly the group waited for us, how one separated from the rest and came forward as a delegate on our nearer approach to hear the news, and how, when she had learned the name of the injured man and that he was none of their people, there came first a natural "Thank God" before she went on to ask us how he was and whether there was good hope of his recovery.'[13]

Stevenson noted that landing on Dhu Heartach was so difficult that the completed lighthouse was routinely to stock six months' worth of provisions. A decade and a half later, in his novel *Kidnapped* (1886), Stevenson shipwrecked David Balfour, his young hero, on the Torran Rocks, then stranded him on Erraid.

Like David Balfour, Robert Louis Stevenson escaped Erraid. He finished his engineering education, and even presented a paper to the Royal Scottish Society of Arts – 'On a New Form of Intermittent Light For Lighthouses'[14] – for which the Society awarded him a silver medal. But, by the time the Dhu Heartach light finally blazed, in 1872, Stevenson had given up a lighthouse career. The

---

[13] Stevenson, Robert Louis, *The New Lighthouse on the Dhu Heartach Rock, Argyllshire*, p15.
[14] Stevenson, Robert Louis, 'On a New Form of Intermittent Light for Lighthouses', in *The Works of Robert Louis Stevenson*, Appendix, pp8-12.

occupation's necessary transition from 'a memory full of ships, and seas, and perilous headlands, and the shining pharos' to 'the petty niceties of drawing [...] several pages of consecutive figures' proved too violent a swell. The engineer was obliged to 'balance one part of genuine life against two parts of drudgery between four walls, and for the sake of the one, manfully accept the other.'[15]

Stevenson traced his transition from lighthouses to literature in a two-part poem, titled 'The Light-Keeper.' In the first part, written in 1869 – just before the 19-year-old Stevenson, still hovering between callings, joined his grandfather on official inspection visits to lighthouses in the Orkney and Shetland islands – Stevenson puts himself into the mind of the keeper, sitting 'within a blaze of light / Held high above the dusky sea', riding out the night until the morning sun gradually illuminates the lighthouse and its surroundings in a series of richly descriptive images. In the second part, written a year later, Stevenson seems to wryly assess his earlier effort: 'Poetry cunningly gilds / The life of the Light-Keeper,' romanticising a figure who remains, nevertheless, an employee. 'This is the man,' Stevenson writes, 'Who gives up all that is lovely in living / For the means to live':

> 'The Poet, deep in a sonnet,
> Numbers his inky fingers
> Fitly to praise him;
> Only we behold him,
> Sitting, patient and stolid,

---

[15] Stevenson, Robert Louis, 'The Education of an Engineer', *Scribner's Magazine*, vol IV no 5, November 1888, p639.

Martyr to a salary.'[16]

The poem reads like Stevenson's warning to himself, the dull light of the keeper's routine guiding him away from the perils of drudgery.

In 1896, two years after Stevenson's death on Upolo, workers under the supervision of his cousin David Alan Stevenson started hauling materials up the 150-foot cliff face of Eilean Mòr, the largest of the Flannan Isles' seven rocky outcrops in the Outer Hebrides. The Flannan Isles lighthouse, finished in 1899, was another Stevenson family triumph, though by now the feat had grown common enough to be taken for granted. But a year after the light opened, on Boxing Day, 1900, the lighthouse ship *Hesperus* arrived at Eilean Mòr and discovered that the three keepers had vanished without a trace. The disappearance was a profound shock to the fraternity of lighthouse builders and keepers, a reminder of the inherent danger of their trade – a danger shrouded, perhaps, by a century of engineering diligence. In his ballad of the Flannan Isles keepers, Wilfrid Wilson Gibson felt the need to enclose and contain the event by imagining the place to be cursed:

> 'We thought how ill-chance came to all
> Who kept the Flannan Light:
> And how the rock had been the death
> Of many a likely lad...'[17]

---

[16] Stevenson, Robert Louis, 'The Light-Keeper', in *The Works of Robert Louis Stevenson*, Appendix, pp25-26.
[17] Gibson, Wilfrid Wilson, 'Flannan Isle', in *Fires*, p47.

Fang Rock is an English location. The Doctor has aimed the TARDIS for the resort town of Brighton, on England's southern coast; Palmerdale's party is en route from the French coastal resort of Deauville to Southampton – a north-by-northwest voyage across the English Channel. The 'Fang Rock' name was probably inspired by Wolf Rock, a lighthouse eight miles off the tip of Cornwall.

The Stevensons built their lighthouses in Scotland, some 300 miles to the north of Fang Rock's presumed location. Fang Rock's construction and operation would have been under the purview of Trinity House, the royally-chartered corporation in charge of lighthouses in England, Wales, the Channel Islands and Gibraltar. Still, Fang Rock's perilous isolation parallels that of Dhu Heartach. The name could also echo that of Bell Rock, the foundation of the family expertise; according to Reuben, the senior member of the Fang Rock crew, the lighthouse has been there for at least 80 years, making it of similar vintage as the Bell Rock light. And the fate of its occupants is explicitly linked to the Flannan Isles light by the Doctor, who quotes Wilfred Wilson Gibson's ballad at story's end. One could be forgiven for imagining that Robert Louis Stevenson's relatives had some professional familiarity with the design and construction of the Fang Rock light.

And now, Fang Rock hosts a visitor not unlike Robert Louis Stevenson, a planner and inventor seduced away from the drawing board by the narrative possibilities of the horizon. Upon meeting Vince, the tyro of the lighthouse crew, the Doctor describes himself twice. 'We're mislaid mariners,' he says, introducing himself and Leela. But then, soon after, the Doctor admits to another persona:

'I'm something of an engineer myself.'[18] The Doctor neatly circumscribes his character: adventurer and architect; servant of chance and savant of technology; master and plaything of space and time; and − in a way Robert Louis Stevenson would have recognised − always at home, and never at home.

2.

For all its period-piece Edwardian atmosphere, *Horror of Fang Rock* is a story about technology − more specifically, the failure of technology. The Rutan's ship crashes; the TARDIS navigation system sends the Doctor and Leela astray; Palmerdale's vessel is dashed against the rocks. Lighthouse technology proves similarly capricious. The newly-electrified carbon arc lamp suddenly turns fickle. The generator that powers the lamp − Ben's métier − recharges the Rutan's lethal powers. A wireless telegraph that might bring help is sabotaged because of its threat to the social order. All of these technologies encode narratives of their own.

The creators of the *Fang Rock* narrative gleaned at least some of their technological knowledge from children's books. (This was not the only **Doctor Who** story thus realised. Long-time **Who** producer Barry Letts routinely advised writers to head to the children's section of the library for research, according to *Fang Rock* writer Terrance Dicks: 'Almost everything you'll want is there, and usually in a simpler, more concise and more visual form than anything you'd be likely to find in the Adult Section.'[19]) One particular book utilised by Dicks and the production crew was *Lighthouses,*

---

[18] Episode 1.
[19] Dicks, Terrance, 'The Script Mutations', *In-Vision* #24, p10.

Lightships and Buoys, a thin 1966 volume by EG Jerrome, a junior school headmaster[20]. That pedigree comes out in Jerrome's writing: the basic facts are laid out in unadorned language, periodically salted with questions to spark young minds: 'Lighthouses out at sea are usually called "rock lighthouses". It is very difficult to build a rock lighthouse. Can you think why?'[21]

A two-page-tall illustration of a typical lighthouse probably played a part in fashioning the look of *Fang Rock*, and Jerrome's detailing of the light-flashing pattern at the Wolf Rock lighthouse might well have helped inspire Fang Rock's name. Indeed, reading the book is like ticking off a list of *Fang Rock*'s plot points – and technologies. There's the lantern ('Men have always tried to make the light as strong as possible'). There's the foghorn ('Fog signals make a deep wailing sound, each lighthouse being different from the next'). There's the telegraph that Skinsale destroys ('Some lighthouses have a wireless room with a radio set or even television for the keepers'). Having listed all that, Jerrome then turns his attention to the one remaining technology in the lighthouse:

> 'The keepers who work on a rock lighthouse lead a lonely life. There are three keepers on the rock at any one time.'

'A rock keeper must be able to do all kinds of jobs,' Jerrome goes on. 'He cannot call someone in to put things right.'[22]

3.

Like a comet, or an asteroid, or a rogue piece of space junk, the

---

[20] 'Production', *In-Vision* #24, p10.
[21] Jerrome, EG, *Lighthouses, Lightships and Buoys*, p10.
[22] Jerrome, *Lighthouses, Lightships and Buoys*, pp22, 30, 19, 32.

arrival on Fang Rock of extraterrestrials – both of them – disrupts a delicate but steady orbital system. British lighthouses had been manned by three-keeper crews since the early 19th century, supposedly after a grim episode at the Smalls lighthouse off the coast of Wales:

> 'It is said that early in the present century, and in a stormy winter of peculiar severity, the light-keepers were deprived of all communication with the land for a period of four months. It was in vain that ships were dispatched towards the rocks; a raging sea invariably prevented their approach. One of them returned, on a certain occasion, with the singular intelligence that her crew had observed a man standing upright and motionless, in a corner of the outer gallery, with a flag of distress floating beside him.'[23]

The seeming sentinel was actually the corpse of Thomas Griffith, who, along with Thomas Howell, had been minding the Smalls light. Griffith's death was accidental, but the relationship between Griffith and Howell had been so notoriously contentious that the latter feared being accused of murder if he cast Griffith's body into the sea; instead, Howell lashed the body to the outside of the building, avoiding contaminating the quarters with the effects of putrefaction while (more or less) preserving evidence of a natural death for any inquisitive coroner. Howells singlehandedly maintained the light until relief could finally arrive – all the while, it is said, haunted by Griffith's lifeless arm, which had come loose

---

[23] WH Davenport Adams, *Lighthouses and Lightships: A Descriptive and Historical Account of Their Mode of Construction and Organization*, pp137-38.

from the restraints and, in the powerful winds, appeared to be waving at the window, beckoning Howells outside. The Gothic overtones of the Smalls incident may have been au courant, but authorities preferred dull security, and three-man crews became the rule.

The third wheel added stability: given the constrained circumstances – all-male crews, shut away for months at a time, often under appallingly harsh conditions – it is surprising how few crews broke down under the pressure. Most, facile or fractious, found an equilibrium. For all its keepers' points of friction, Fang Rock seems to be no exception. Reuben and Ben bicker over the advantages of oil-fired and electrical lights, but the two quietly but firmly defend the light's operation from their perception of Vince's inexperience ('After all,' Ben says, 'the boy's only learning'), and it is telling that, for all his mistrust of electricity, Reuben's intuition is that Ben's death is no accident ('Ben knew every blessed inch of that there machine'). Vince, for his part, is the natural target of the older keepers' jesting, but is comfortable enough to give it back on occasion.

Given the science-fiction setting, the Fang Rock ménage suggests that classic conundrum of celestial mechanics, the three-body problem. The problem, though, had long been of maritime concern as well. Calculating the relative motion of three celestial bodies under the gravitational influence of each other – the archetypal example being the Earth, the Moon, and the Sun – became a task of seagoing navigators, who, during the 18th and 19th centuries, determined longitude by measuring the positions of the moon and other night-sky objects, then comparing those positions to a theoretical model of the moon's position to calculate the exact time relative to a standard (Greenwich Mean Time, for instance). The time could only be as accurate as the theory, making the small wobbles in the gravitational dance between earth, moon, and sun loom surprisingly large.

The development of the marine chronometer, its complex clockwork compensating for changes in conditions and temperature, made the three-body problem moot for marine navigation, but space travel revived it. Figuring out where a given orb in the sky should be at a given time, once necessary to match up observation with almanac, now held the higher stakes of guiding spacecraft to a celestial body. The Doctor's missing of Brighton, for example, could have resulted from a slightly too casual calculation of the pertinent three-body problem.

The three-body problem has no general algebraic solution. Like the lighthouse crews, every triangulation requires its own idiosyncratic calculation. *Horror of Fang Rock* could have generated easy dramatic tension by having the three keepers at each others' throats. Instead, the crew is stereotypical but accurate: stock characters, contrasting types, but committed, by habit and professionalism, to cooperation. The story is thus set up not as just another fraught situation for the Doctor to resolve, but as a revelation of the Doctor's true nature. Instead of stabilising a volatile situation, the Doctor is a competing centre of gravity, forever pulling crisis into the orbital system, throwing off all the maths.

By most accounts, this was an effect experienced in real time during the making of *Fang Rock*. The crew manning the Fang Rock light is like a blurry reflection of the production crew. Vince, inexperienced but eager, might be novice producer Graham Williams, learning the job in an isolated location. Ben's technical diligence could find its parallel in director Paddy Russell, competently persevering through what was, by all accounts, a stressful shoot. (Russell's resentment at the effort of managing Tom Baker's imperious working habits made it her last **Doctor Who** effort.) And Reuben, the superstitious old-timer? Perhaps Robert Holmes, the script editor, both source and sceptic of a wide swath of **Doctor Who** history and lore; or perhaps Terrance Dicks, the script's author, also a ubiquitous writerly presence among **Doctor Who**, particularly through his prolific novelisations: a repository of fantastic tales retold. Or, perhaps, both. (Reuben's corporeal form, after all, ends up hosting two distinct consciousnesses.) And the entire mechanism has to make room for Tom Baker's increasingly capricious and curt characterisation of the Doctor, a mass that will perturb the whole trajectory of the series.

4.

That the Fang Rock light is an electric carbon arc lamp indicates something about the lighthouse and its location. The earliest lighthouses generated light with bonfires, coal braziers, or candles – the last being the choice of Henry Winstanley, who built a lighthouse on the Eddystone Rocks off the coast of Cornwall, the first lighthouse to be erected in the open sea. That lighthouse collapsed in the Great Storm of 1703, an unusually fierce cyclone that also claimed 13 Royal Navy vessels. Winstanley was at the Eddystone light, making repairs, when the storm hit; he and five other crew perished. (The Doctor's mocking Reuben's possible preference for 'a really large candle,' rather than being a reduction to absurdity, instead suggests that the old-timer's conservatism can be measured in centuries[24].) By the mid-1800s, oil lamps were standard, fuelled by rendered whale blubber and, later, mineral oil. Gas lighting was introduced in 1865 when John Wigham installed his lamp in the Baily Lighthouse in Dublin.

Still, the potential of the carbon arc lamp – an electric current jumping the distance between two carbon electrodes, producing a brilliant blaze – was tantalising. The lamp's invention is usually attributed to Sir Humphry Davy, whose interest in electrified light was preceded by inquiries into trippier forms of illumination. In 1799, at the age of 20, having obtained his first real scientific post – at the Pneumatic Institution, a recently-founded laboratory investigating the medical use of various gases[25] – Davy began researching the effects of nitrous oxide: laughing gas. He experimentally ascertained its composition and chemical properties, then administered the gas to all manner of animals, observing its varied and often fatal effects. He then experimented on himself:

> 'The first feelings... were succeeded by a sensation analogous to gentle pressure on all the muscles, attended by an highly pleasurable thrilling, particularly in the chest and the extremities... [A]t last an irresistible propensity to action was indulged in; I recollect but indistinctly what followed; I know that my motions were various and

---

[24] Episode 1.

[25] On Davy and the Institution, see West, John B, 'Humphry Davy, Nitrous Oxide, the Pneumatic Institution, and the Royal Institution', *American Journal of Physiology: Lung Cellular and Molecular Physiology*, pp661-67.

violent.'[26]

James Watt – another habitué of the Pneumatic Institution, fresh off a long round of patent litigation over his steam engine – built Davy an airtight box, large enough in which to sit, that he might administer the gas to famous friends and acquaintances and collect their impressions. Among them was Peter Mark Roget, later to compile his eponymous thesaurus. 'Thoughts rushed like a torrent through my mind,' Roget reported, with appropriate description, 'as if their velocity had been suddenly accelerated by the bursting of a barrier.'[27]

The laughing gas experiments, however, instilled in Davy something of a taste for life on the edge. He began testing other gases, again using himself as a guinea pig, often to harrowing effect. An attempt at breathing nitric oxide went awry when the gas, combining with air as Davy inhaled, turned to nitric acid, severely burning the inside of his mouth. (Only Davy's habit of flushing his lungs with laughing gas prevented his lungs from being fatally burned.) Undeterred, Davy resolved to be the first to breathe 'pure hydrocarbonate gas' – carbon monoxide.

> 'The first inspiration produced a sort of numbness and loss of feeling in the chest and about the pectoral muscles. After the second inspiration, I lost all power of perceiving external things, and had no distinct sensation except a terrible oppression on the chest. During the third expiration, this

---

[26] Davy, Humphry, *Researches, Chemical and Philosophical: Chiefly Concerning Nitrous Oxide, or Dephlogisticated Nitrous Air, and Its Respiration*, pp457-58.
[27] Davy, *Researches*, pp510-11.

feeling disappeared, I seemed sinking into annihilation, and had just power enough to drop the mouth-piece from my unclosed lips. A short interval must have passed during which I respired common air, before the objects about me were distinguishable. On recollecting myself, I faintly articulated, "I do not think I shall die."[28]

Such reckless zeal for knowledge starts to feel more than a bit familiar. The impulsive experimentation, the breezy cocksureness with which he puts himself in harm's way, the objective observation of his own peril: Davy's scientific tendencies echo those of a certain renegade Time Lord. ('Is this advisable?' Skinsale asks, as the Doctor puts a plan into action. 'Probably not,' the Doctor admits[29].) Davy's shift of focus to electricity – its own dangers notwithstanding – could be considered prudent in comparison.

Around 1800, Davy built a replica of Alessandro Volta's voltaic pile and started running electricity through all kinds of substances to see if the current would decompose them into their constituent parts. Along the way, he discovered that electricity would jump across a gap between two bits of the same element, producing a spark, and that the colour and intensity of the spark changed from element to element. Carbon sparked particularly bright; and, sometime in the next few years, Davy massaged that spark into a consistent flame. In 1808, a private subscription was organised to raise enough money for Davy to build a much larger, 2,000-cell battery, which he used to demonstrate the new light, arching

---

[28] Davy, *Researches*, pp468-69.
[29] Episode 4.

between two carbon electrodes[30].

But battery-powered lamps were impractical for lighthouses. Throughout the 19th century, the course of lighthouse evolution would be slowed not by any lack of innovation in illumination techniques, but by the difficulty of providing the necessary infrastructure. The carbon arc was not the first example. After seeing Michael Faraday, Davy's protégé, direct a flame fuelled by oxygen and hydrogen at a block of quicklime, producing a formidably bright light, a Scottish engineer named Thomas Drummond scaled the demonstration up into a practical application. A demonstration for Trinity House yielded impressive results, the new light casting night-time shadows at a distance of 10 miles. But it required a steady stream of its two gaseous fuels, and the brick channels that would supply it repeatedly leaked. Limelight instead found its home in the theatre.

Similarly, Davy's carbon arc blaze remained a curiosity until generator design caught up with the light's appetite for electricity. Faraday was behind the first experiments. The father of electrochemistry and the inventor of the generator also maintained a keen interest in boats and lighthouses, doing important work for Trinity House. In December 1858, Faraday and Frederick Hale Holmes, who had been experimenting with generators on his own, installed a carbon arc lamp in the lighthouse at South Foreland, just north of Dover; by the following spring, it was running continuously. 'The light produced is powerful beyond any other

---

[30] For an attempt to pin down the chronology of the arc lamp's development, see Thompson, Silvanus P, 'The Arc Light' (I), pp943-46.

that I have yet seen so applied,' Faraday reported, 'and in principle may be accumulated to any degree.'[31] But it was still an expensive way to signal ships; the South Foreland light soon reverted to oil, and would not install a permanent electric light until the 1870s.

By then, Faraday's rotating-disc generator had been superseded by dynamos, which spun coils of wire through electrically-generated magnetic fields. The first practical examples all appeared in the winter of 1866-67, independently invented by English polymath Charles Wheatstone, his engineering countryman Samuel Varley, and the German industrialist Werner von Siemens. As dynamos changed the cost of steady sufficient power from prohibitively expensive to merely very expensive, electric lights made tentative inroads, though not without controversy. In particular, naysayers insisted that, despite the electric lamp's greater candlepower, its supposed tilt toward the violet end of the spectrum rendered it less effective in heavy fog. (Reuben agrees: 'Another thing with oil, it gives a better light in fog.'[32])

Finally, in 1884, a committee convened by Trinity House, numbering among its advisors most of the leading lighthouse engineers of the day (including Robert Louis Stevenson's father, Thomas), built three temporary lighthouses at South Foreland – one for oil, one for gas, one for electricity – in order to more rigorously test the performance of each type of illumination. 'The electric light,' reported one source, 'was demonstrated to be the

---

[31] *Report of the Commissioners Appointed to Inquire into the Condition and Management of Lights, Buoys, and Beacons*, Appendix, p3.
[32] Episode 1.

most powerful of the luminaries, not only in clear weather, but also in haze, mist, rain or snow; and has, to a limited extent, even greater penetration in actual fog.'[33] Still, the expense caused the committee to recommend carbon arc lamps only in those lights where the lack of visibility and danger were critical. Fang Rock's electric light is testament to its peril.

The dynamos that powered the first lighthouse lamps were behemoths: coal-fired, steam-driven giants often relegated to their own buildings. Despite the dynamo's joint English-German parentage, it was a Parisian that won the early race for market share. Baron Auguste de Méritens devised crucial improvements to dynamo design that made his machines the standard for lighthouses installed with carbon arc lamps. (De Méritens' interest in Davy's arc went beyond light: in 1881, he was granted a patent for arc welding as well.) De Méritens alternating-current magnetos ran the electric lamp in those 1884 tests at South Foreland, and were installed in many lighthouses over the next few years.

The equipment in the Fang Rock generator room is from the next generation: still run by steam, but with considerably less footprint – small enough to fit snugly (and, from a narrative standpoint, conveniently) in the lighthouse itself. Technology changes; but greed and folly endure. By the advent of the Edwardian era, de Méritens himself was gone. In 1896, his arc-welding patent expired, and his apparently precarious fortune evaporated. Two years later, in a cottage in the Parisian suburb of Éragny, his debts caught up with him. The final blow was the repossession of his

---

[33] Williams, Thomas, *Life of Sir James Nicholas Douglass FRS, &c, &c (Formerly Engineer-in-Chief to the Trinity House)*, pp157-58.

furniture; after sending a friendly editor a thoroughly anti-Semitic suicide note blaming 'Jewish France' for his downfall, de Méritens and his wife drank poison and died[34].

One thinks of Palmerdale's desperation to reach London in time to make a killing, or Skinsale's anxiety over his honour and reputation – anxiety that, however unwittingly, prompts him to suicidal action, destroying the wireless transmitter that might have brought help. Victorian and Edwardian technology could make fortunes; but such wealth and status were, perhaps, more precarious than they seemed.

5.

The diamonds that Palmerdale carries are his security against the loss of status – 'his insurance,' Skinsale notes. The Doctor, characteristically, embeds Palmerdale's diamonds in the lighthouse's mesh of technology, using the largest as a 'focusing device' in the 'amplified carbon oscillator' he improvises out of the arc lamp's beam of light[35]. In putting the largest of Palmerdale's diamonds in proximity with the carbon arc lamp, the Doctor harkens back to Humphry Davy and his early chemical investigations. As Davy noted,

> 'If it should be ultimately found that the diamond is merely pure carbon, it will be an argument in favour of the varieties

---

[34] Both the details of De Méritens' death and his note were reported in the equally anti-Semitic Lyon newspaper *La France Libre* on November 4, 1898, under the headline 'Suicide d'un Inventeur'.

[35] Episode 4.

of elementary forms being produced by different aggregations or arrangements of particles of the same matter; for it is scarcely possible to fix upon bodies less analogous than lamp black, and the most perfect and beautiful of the gems.'[36]

How exactly the Doctor converts the incoherent light of the lamp into a coherent laser-like beam is left unsaid. If he were building a standard laser, he might use the diamond as a so-called 'gain medium'. When electromagnetic radiation – in the form, perhaps, of the carbon arc's light – is pumped into a diamond, some of the diamond's electrons will absorb a photon and be bumped into a higher-energy state; an electron in that excited state can be knocked backed down to a lower energy level by another passing photon, in the process emitting a second photon going with the same direction and energy. It's like shooting an arrow at a cocked crossbow in a way that results in both arrow and crossbow bolt flying toward the same target. If you can coax the majority of the diamond's electrons into firing extra photon-arrows, then the diamond will emit more photons than it absorbs – the light amplification that accounts for two-fifths of the laser ('light amplification by stimulated emission of radiation') acronym.

But the diamond-as-focusing-device detail – virtually the only thing we learn about the Doctor's apparatus – hints at something closer to a Raman laser. In 1928, Chandrasekhara Venkata Raman gave a lecture in Bangalore describing what was later dubbed Raman scattering, a phenomenon in which the photon absorption-

---

[36] Davy, Humphry, *The Collected Works of Sir Humphry Davy, vol IV: Elements of Chemical Philosophy*, p231.

emission two-step is **inelastic**: an electron absorbs a photon of a certain frequency and energy, but emits a photon of a different frequency and energy[37]. Raman scattering can be triggered by sending laser light through a transparent medium, which alters the light's frequency by a fixed amount; in practical terms, one can combine different lasers and different media to generate laser light at whatever frequency one might want. In addition, the effect can be exploited to combine multiple input beams into a single amplified output. And, it turns out, diamonds are unusually good for this. In 2016, Rich Mildren and the Diamond Laser Group at Macquarie University were able to use a diamond to combine three beams into a single, high-power output with significant efficiency. '[D]iamond,' the group concluded, 'is a promising solid-state material for enabling combination of high-power beams via the Raman nonlinear interaction.'[38] The Doctor may have got a century's jump on diamond laser technology.

But what about the oscillating part? Carbon arc lamps did oscillate; in fact, they were annoyingly noisy. Streetlamps were constantly humming; other arc lights would hiss or squawk. Trying to isolate the problem, William Duddell, an English engineer, found that a modulated voltage control would allow the arc to produce musical tones. A 1901 *New York Times* report on Duddell's demonstrations raised the possibility of, say, all the streetlights in New York City

---

[37] Raman, CV, 'A New Radiation', *Indian Journal of Physics*, pp387-98.
[38] Mildren, Richard, Aaron McKay, Ondrej Kitzler, Robert Williams, David Spence and David Coutts, 'Diamond Enables Combination of Non-Collinear Kilowatt Beams', *SPIE Newsroom*, 29 September 2016.

joining together in a single melody: 'As an enthusiastic scientist has put it, the time is perhaps not far distant when we shall be able to realise something of the grandeur of "the morning stars singing together."'[39]

Duddell's focus on novelty, though, missed the true importance of a modulated, voltage-controlled electric arc. Instead, it was a Danish engineer, Valdemar Poulson, who made the connection with another cutting-edge technology: the arc could be used as a radio transmitter. The Poulson arc first demonstrated the practicality of continuous-wave radio transmission, which would lay the groundwork for audio radio broadcasting. Davy's carbon arc, at several iterations' remove from its bright origins, helped make wireless ubiquitous.

6.

South Foreland, where Faraday and Holmes first demonstrated the potential of the carbon arc lamp, was where the wireless telegraph found its place in the lighthouse as well. On Christmas Eve 1898, Guglielmo Marconi demonstrated the feasibility of wireless ship-to-shore telegraphy between the East Goodwin lightship, 12 miles off the coast, and the South Foreland light. The aerial Marconi built on shore was far bigger than it needed to be: he was also testing communication across the English Channel, back and forth between England and France. He already anticipated building a worldwide network.

---

[39] 'Music in Electric Arcs: An English Physicist, with Shunt Circuit and Keyboard, Made Them Play Tunes', *New York Times*; Crab, Simon, 'The "Singing Arc": William Duddell, UK, 1899'.

The father of wireless had a talent for attracting patronage and publicity. Marconi moved comfortably in English circles; his mother was Scotch-Irish – the granddaughter of the founder of the Jameson whiskey distillery – and the young Guglielmo spent part of his childhood in Bedford. Many of his early demonstrations of wireless technology were hung on various attention-grabbing hooks. Marconi mounted a transmitter on the mast of a ship and wired live updates from the Kingstown Regatta to the *Daily Express* newspaper of Dublin in time for the evening editions. He established a link between the royal yacht, moored off the Isle of Wight, and Osborne House on the shore, so that Queen Victoria could check in on the Prince of Wales, who was recovering from a fractured knee-cap. Some of the earliest wireless messages were banal medical updates:

'August 4th.

'From Dr Fripp to Sir James Reid.

'H.R.H. The Prince of Wales has passed another excellent night, and is in very good spirits and health. The knee is most satisfactory.'[40]

After the South Foreland demonstrations, the potential for Marconi's technology to save seagoing lives was immediately recognised, if not immediately implemented. In 1900, when the Association of the Chambers of Commerce of the United Kingdom held its autumn meeting, a resolution was passed urging such wireless connections promptly be installed across Britain. The

---

[40] Marconi, Guglielmo, 'Wireless Telegraphy', *The Electrician* #1086, 10 March 1899, p694.

sense was that Trinity House was dragging its heels, according to Ben Nicholson, yacht designer for the firm of Camper and Nicholsons, which built some of the era's most luxurious launches:

> 'Mr NICHOLSON (Portsmouth) said that his friend Mr Bayly had spent a large amount of time and money in urging the Trinity House authorities to take up the question. He was particularly urged to further endeavours by the fact of three ships being wrecked in a snowstorm off the Start Lighthouse. He saw those wrecks himself, and had been assured that twenty-three men were drowned under the eyes of the men in the lighthouse, because they had no means of communicating with the lifeboat station [...] There was no possibility of rescuing the crew simply because Trinity House or the Board of Trade had persistently refused to adopt the communication which the Resolution suggested.'[41]

Apparently Fang Rock lacks a lifeboat station, to judge by the absence of a wireless message after the wreck of Palmerdale's yacht – a yacht that could very possibly have come out of the Camper and Nicholsons' shipyard.

Just like the electric lamp, Reuben is dismissive of the wireless telegraph.

DOCTOR

Shouldn't you be using it to report Ben's death?

---

[41] *The Chamber of Commerce Journal*, October 1900 Supplement, p21.

REUBEN

Wireless won't bring Ben back, will it?[42]

(In the novelisation, the Doctor theorises that Reuben, in spite of insisting to the contrary, does not actually know how to use the device[43].) Reuben instead will send a message to shore via semaphore the next day. Whether this is semaphore by flag or flashing light, we are not told – though, given Reuben's preference for 'the old days,' flag would be a good guess. Either way, Reuben would, possibly, turn to the International Code of Signals, as published by the British Board of Trade. He could use the Condensed Code: three- or four-letter groups standing in for hundreds of common messages. In this case, he might send signals to shore thus: DWM ('Dead. Died'); DWN ('Accident'); DJR ('I am short manned')[44].

Palmerdale, though, is eager to use the Marconi apparatus; it is his best chance at contacting his London brokers. Wireless communication of financial information would have been a novelty at the time. Radio had little effect on the mechanism of trading, simply because the infrastructure of telegraphy-by-wire was already so extensively ingrained in the financial system. An unscrupulous trader looking to make a killing would have been hard-pressed to find a situation where Marconi's radio would yield an appreciable advantage. Marconi's invention certainly made a splash in the markets: wireless-telegraphy-stock schemes and

---

[42] Episode 1.

[43] Dicks, Terrance, *Doctor Who and the Horror of Fang Rock*, p32.

[44] *The International Code of Signals for the Use of All Nations: Prepared Under the Authority of the Board of Trade*, pp17, 20.

frauds would suffuse stock markets for most of the first decade of the 20th century. But the ability of the technology itself to enable trading shenanigans was limited.

Marconi, born into wealth, made another fortune off the back of wireless; but his roving eye and workaholic tendencies combined to sink his first marriage, to the former Beatrice O'Brien, a daughter of the Irish aristocracy. Before the final break, a friend of the family made a last-ditch attempt to salvage the relationship, taking Beatrice and her children to Houlgate, a resort town on the Normandy coast, in hope that Marconi, then busy in England, would more easily find time to be with his family. But Marconi only rarely showed up, and, as his daughter Degna remembered it, Houlgate was 'dull, cold, and grey'. So, the group decamped for a more glittering locale, one familiar to Palmerdale and his coterie: Deauville. The casino and social whirl did little to lift Beatrice's mood, but Degna and her siblings, at least, were able to skate by on reputation where sound engineering failed:

> 'The brightest moment of our stay from my standpoint was when the proprietor of our hotel, a vast, charmless pile fronting the beach, offered prizes for the handsomest sand castles [...] Some of the other children's castles were far sturdier and more ambitious than ours but the prizegiver was Italian and what is more a devotee of Father's. We could not have lost if we had tried.'[45]

Back on Fang Rock, the Rutan's improvised transmitter is just good enough to hail its own compatriots. The power relay and signal

---

[45] Marconi, Degna, *My Father Marconi*, pp239-40.

modulator are alien, a remote but parallel evolution of the same principles Marconi harnessed. But the power itself is Edwardian, supplied by Fang Rock's generator. Nevertheless, the Rutan is able to expropriate it, turning it to other, unintended purposes. In doing so, the Rutan has done its part to sustain another old maritime tradition: scavenging.

7.

Robert Louis Stevenson recalled stories that his illustrious grandfather told of Sanday and Ronaldsay, two of the Orkney islands off Scotland's northern coast. The elder Robert Stevenson had helped his stepfather build a lighthouse on Ronaldsay, then returned to Sanday to construct the Start Point lighthouse, which was completed in 1806. The islanders were farmers and sheepherders, but the lights eliminated what had been, for centuries, a prized source of side income: scavenging goods and materials from the many ships wrecked off the islands' shores. The practice, practical and ruthless, shaped the islands in more ways than one: 'the inhabitants have certainly had their share of wrecked goods, for the eye is presented with these melancholy remains in almost every form,' as Stevenson told it. On one of his surveying and inspection visits, Stevenson saw a meadow 'paled round chiefly with cedar-wood and mahogany from the wreck of a Honduras-built ship.' The destruction of a ship 'laden with wine' led to islanders drinking fine claret with their breakfast porridge. Having hired a local to pilot him around the islands on his boat, Stevenson noticed the poor quality of the sails, and pointed it out. 'Had it been His will that you came na' here wi' your lights,' the skipper replied, 'we might 'a' had better sails to our boats, and more o' other things.'[46]

The matrix of technology that is the Fang Rock lighthouse, a secular temple to safety and navigation, becomes, in the space of a couple of hours, the site of two wrecks and one craft blown significantly off course. In a curious reversal, it is the stranded who begin to scavenge. Palmerdale and his party begin to forage for deference and comfort, demanding brandy, clean clothes, bedding. ('Trouble with the gentry,' Reuben grumbles, 'they always want running after.'[47]) In addition to its distress beacon, the Rutan is after bodies and energy, looking to salvage the earth into a military waystation – and cannon fodder for its enemies.

The Doctor does his own scavenging: the gunpowder from signal rockets, a launcher converted into a cannon, various found objects – 'an assortment of rusty tins, filled with nuts and bolts, nails, cogs and other engineering debris'[48] – as shrapnel. Davy's carbon-arc lamp is weaponised via Palmerdale's diamonds. The Doctor's recycling is not mercenary; it is all about – well, let him tell it:

SKINSALE

What's all this about, Doctor?

DOCTOR

Survival, Colonel.

---

[46] Stevenson, 'Records of a Family of Engineers', pp244-45.
[47] Episode 2.
[48] Dicks, *Doctor Who and the Horror of Fang Rock*, pp113-14.

SKINSALE

Survival?

DOCTOR

Yes. Yours, mine, all of us.[49]

But the residents of Sanday and Ronaldsay led a precarious existence, too; scavenging shipwrecks helped them survive.

And, like the islanders, the Doctor approaches his task without much pause for sentiment. While the fate of humankind is paramount in his mind, the fates of individual humans, by the end, make hardly an emotional dent. On Sanday and Ronaldsay, Robert Louis Stevenson surmised, such indifference was characteristic of secluded, tightly-bound communities: 'The danger is to those from without, who have not grown up from childhood in these islands, but appear suddenly in that narrow horizon, life-sized apparitions... [N]o feeling of kinship is awakened by their peril.'[50] For those who live on the edge – of the sea, of the universe, of life – peril is an everyday part of the landscape. Storms rise; fog rolls in; ships run aground; aliens land.

'It is not wickedness,' Stevenson concluded, 'it is scarce evil; it is only, in its highest power, the sense of isolation and the wise disinterestedness' of such outmost residents. And so the islanders 'will assist at a shipwreck [...] and when the fatal scene is over, and the beach strewn with dead bodies, they will fence their fields with

---

[49] Episode 3.
[50] Stevenson, 'Records of a Family of Engineers', p246.

mahogany, and, after a decent grace, sup claret to their porridge.'[51] For all his compassion, the Doctor exhibits more than a little of such pragmatism. The only difference might be that he is rarely afforded the opportunity for a decent grace. As Stevenson put it in his poetry, the Doctor must often ignore all that is lovely in living in favour of engineering the means to live.

8.

In other words, the Doctor rarely has time for sentiment – which brings up one last technology, the manipulation of the elements of the TARDIS's acronym: time and relative dimensions in space. The TARDIS's capabilities both do and do not explain the Doctor's presence on Fang Rock, how and why he is there at all. On the surface, *Horror of Fang Rock* presents one of the most bald-faced examples of the Doctor's seeming affinity for tempero-spatial coincidence. With the ability to be anywhere in the universe at any time in its multi-billion-year history, the Doctor just happens to be heading toward the English coast, just at the moment that, very nearby, a single Rutan scout, in the midst of a millennia-long war, happens to crash-land on a small, rocky, out-of-the-way planet.

The Doctor's career suggests more than one possible explanation for this serendipity. The Gallifrey-based Celestial Intervention Agency[52]? Perhaps the Rutan's presence on earth foreshadowed a temporal paradox. (The Sontaran-Rutan war had previously prompted time-travel shenanigans, after all, and would do so

---

[51] Stevenson, 'Records of a Family of Engineers', pp246-47.
[52] Alluded to in *The Deadly Assassin* (1976).

again[53].) Or it might have been the TARDIS itself, sending the Doctor not where he wanted, but where he was needed – as the TARDIS, in temporarily-assumed humanoid form, admitted to a later incarnation of the Doctor[54]. Or maybe it was just the nature of reality: the Doctor did once suggest that coincidences were 'what the universe does for fun.'[55] There are, apparently, mechanisms in place to ensure the Doctor shows up in the right place at the right time.

But it's not **quite** the right time. The Rutan is already ashore. A victim has already been claimed. The fog has descended. The pattern is, rather, that the Doctor arrives in the right place at the time most well-suited to a heroic performance: just after the point when mayhem might have been completely forestalled, but just before things get completely (planetarily, galactically, universally) out of hand. And one has to wonder if that is, on some level, the Doctor's preference. It is allegedly the Doctor's biological imprint that made this TARDIS operable – the so-called 'Rassilon Imprimatur'[56]. A bit of the Doctor's taste for jeopardy may have installed itself in the TARDIS's clockwork.

In fact, the entire Fang Rock affair escalates into the contours of the Doctor's personality – his breezy cockiness ensures his admission to the situation; his lofty, even disdainful intellect finds a stage in his parley with the Rutan; his abrupt confidence in his own

---

[53] As chronicled in *The Time Warrior* (1973-74) and *The Two Doctors* (1985), both written by Robert Holmes.
[54] In *The Doctor's Wife* (2011).
[55] *Closing Time* (2011).
[56] According to *The Two Doctors*.

judgement dooms the lighthouse's inhabitants and visitors; his faith and fluency in technological solutions saves the rest of the planet. And, one suspects, it is a personality shaped by both a reflexive familiarity and affinity for technology and a restless, nomadic attitude toward everything else. One finds a similar character in another peripatetic engineer, one who spent a life sending beacons into the fog and doing his best to avert disaster on the rocks: Thomas Stevenson. When Robert Louis Stevenson eulogised his father, the builder of the Dhu Heartach light, the man he apprenticed with around the coast of Scotland, he described him in terms that might make him the Doctor's long-lost twin:

> 'He was a man of a somewhat antique strain: [...] with a profound essential melancholy of disposition and (what often accompanies it) the most humorous geniality in company; shrewd and childish; passionately attached, passionately prejudiced; a man of many extremes, many faults of temper, and no very stable foothold for himself among life's troubles. Yet he was a wise adviser; many men, and these not inconsiderable, took counsel with him habitually.'[57]

Both thrive on the most fraught situations – when the problem is acute, the odds longest, the difficulty most profound. The only difference is how that manifests in time. Thomas Stevenson, the diligent planner, would spend years on a single, barren rock. The Doctor, who, like Thomas Stevenson's son, abandoned such diligence for more swashbuckling roving, arrives just in the nick of time – which, of course, means that the time for a calm,

---

[57] Stevenson, Robert Louis, *Memories and Portraits*, pp138-39.

methodical resolution has long past. Such is the case at Fang Rock; such is the case in so many similar situations. The Doctor is there, but too late.

PART 2: TIME AND CLASS

'"And that's the end," she said, and she saw in his eyes, as the interest of the story died away in them, something else take its place; something wondering, pale, like the reflection of a light, which at once made him gaze and marvel. Turning, she looked across the bay, and there, sure enough, coming regularly across the waves first two quick strokes and then one long steady stroke, was the light of the Lighthouse. It had been lit.'

[Virginia Woolf, *To the Lighthouse*][58]

1.

From the lighthouse, everything back on shore, including class, seems far away and insignificant. Is that why Virginia Woolf's Charles Tansley persists in mentioning it? 'No going to the lighthouse, James,' he keeps saying, knowing a trip to the lighthouse is all six-year-old James Ramsay wants. Tansley, brittle and smug – 'the little atheist,' the other Ramsay children call him – seems delighted: the scion's desire has been thwarted. The winds are unfavourable. The forces of nature have been drafted into Tansley's ongoing skirmishes of rank and standing. Or is Tansley relieved? The lighthouse is a harsh place, more harsh than the Ramsay's summer home on the Isle of Skye; the lighthouse is a rock against which might be dashed the complex gradations of British class, the fuel of Tansley's burning resentment.

That is how the Ramsay family sees Tansley. He would disagree: his

---

[58] Woolf, Virginia, *To the Lighthouse*, p61.

barely-disguised disdain for the Ramsays' middle-class privilege is his armour against slight, against a society that would deny him opportunity on such arbitrary grounds. And James Ramsay's ire falls not on Tansley, but his father, the philosopher, the disciple of truth and rationality. The winds **are** unfavourable, and no amount of wishing will change them. Charles Tansley would shatter James' privileges, but what does a six-year-old know of privilege? Mr Ramsay, on the other hand, would shatter his children's illusions, and illusions are the wealth of children. 'Had there been an axe handy, or a poker, any weapon that would have gashed a hole in his father's breast and killed him, there and then, James would have seized it.'[59]

Throughout Virginia Woolf's 1927 novel *To the Lighthouse*, such sparks jump the gap between wishful thinking and unforgiving fact, as happens—albeit in less decorous manner—in *Horror of Fang Rock*. James Tansley's youthful fury highlights the divergence: his imaginary violence becomes all too real when the conflict between belief and reality is relocated to the Fang Rock light. But, in one aspect, the stories run parallel: in both, the rifts and frictions are intertwined with the ritual inequities of class.

To the Lighthouse is at least somewhat autobiographical. Woolf modelled the Ramsay parents after her own: Leslie Stephen, a critic and thinker, the first editor of the *Dictionary of National Biography*; and the former Julia Duckworth, a noted beauty and a favourite of the Pre-Raphaelite artists – the model for, among others, the Virgin Mary in Edward Burne-Jones' painting of *The Annunciation*. Her family did rent a summer home on the coast of Cornwall; the place

---

[59] Woolf, *To the Lighthouse*, p4.

did have a lighthouse, Godrevy Lighthouse, some way out to sea. There was a trip to the lighthouse, and a son frustrated at being denied the chance to see it –

> 'On Saturday morning Master Hilary Flint and Master Basil Smith came up to Tolland House and asked Master Thoby and Miss Virginia Stephen to accompany them to the lighthouse as Freeman the boatman said that there was a perfect tide and wind for going there. Master Adrian Stephen was much disappointed at not being allowed to go'

– as reported in the September 12, 1892 issue of the *Hyde Park Gate News*, a handwritten chronicle of family life that the young Virginia and her sister, Vanessa Bell, kept going for four years[60].

The novel transmutes family history into a complex meditation on perception, purpose, and personal awareness. Underneath it all is an inescapable feature of English life: the delicate, dissonant counterpoint of class. The Ramsays mirror Woolf's upper-middle-class upbringing. Charles Tansley, Mr Ramsay's student, has, through work and education, tried to surmount his lower-class origins. Lily Briscoe, an unmarried family friend, a painter, views the Ramsays' middle-class life with a clear and occasionally sceptical eye, but herself is able to pursue her art thanks to her own middle-class status. The Ramsays' servants, Mrs McNab and Mrs Bast, hover in the background for much of the novel, but then, at a crucial point, their consciousness comes to the fore.

And then there are the lighthouse-keepers, the working-class

---

[60] Woolf, Virginia, and Vanessa Bell, '"Hyde Park Gate News", a magazine by Virginia Woolf and Vanessa Bell'.

guardians of the remote, longed-for vision. Mrs Ramsay regards them with condescending charity, knitting a stocking for one keeper's son, gathering up 'whatever she could find lying about, not really wanted, but only littering the room, to give those poor fellows.'[61] And yet, those 'poor fellows' occupy the place symbolising the Ramsays' aspirations, deferred, unreachable. 'So much depends then,' thinks Lily Briscoe, 'upon distance; whether people are near us or far from us'[62]. That distance can be social as well.

2.

Horror of Fang Rock throws together three mutually and fundamentally alien species; namely, the British lower, middle, and upper classes. The habit of class plays a part in deciding more than one character's fate. Harker, confronted by the Rutan-as-Reuben, too readily assumes the security of working-class camaraderie; Adelaide renders herself helpless by conforming to middle-class strictures of feminine propriety; Palmerdale and Skinsale are done in by the cupidity of maintaining their upper-class station. Like the skeletons leading the old Dances of Death, class divisions and expectations guide the Fang Rock Edwardians into fatal traps.

As with so many other factors, the lighthouse setting concentrates and amplifies class divisions. Lighthouses had long hovered in a kind of class limbo, uneasily caught between property and welfare, commerce and charity, elite bounty and egalitarian aid. Early lighthouses were often privately built, protecting fortunes as well

---

[61] Woolf, *To the Lighthouse*, p5.
[62] Woolf, *To the Lighthouse*, p191.

as sailors; Henry Winstanley built his doomed Eddystone light, for instance, after his own merchant vessels were wrecked on the rocks.

Tellingly, rebellious Englishmen across the Atlantic took lighthouses out of private hands. When the first United States Congress met in 1789, the ninth law passed was 'An Act for the establishment and support of Lighthouses, Beacons, Buoys, and Public Piers'. The legislators deemed lighthouses too important to be left up to the individual states, and put them under federal control, 'together with the lands and tenements thereunto belonging, and together with the jurisdiction of the same.'[63] Lighthouses were essential to the new democratic experiment.

By the Victorian era, lighthouses were considered a public good in Britain as well. After Leela smashes down the door to the Fang Rock lighthouse's bunk room, the Doctor's wry aside − 'The Malicious Damage Act of 1861 covers lighthouses' − assumes as much: the Act did not specifically mention damage to lighthouses, but rather to any building 'devoted or dedicated to Public Use or Ornament'[64]. The law did order imprisonment for anyone who would 'unlawfully mask, alter, or remove any Light or Signal [...] tending to the immediate Loss or Destruction of any Ship, Vessel, or Boat'; though he would still have to prove malicious intent, Palmerdale's attempt to affix blame for his yacht's destruction on

---

[63] 'An Act for the Establishment and Support of Lighthouses, Beacons, Buoys, and Public Piers' (US 1 Stat. 53–54 [7 Aug. 1789]).
[64] Episode 3; 'An Act to consolidate and amend the Statute Law of England and Ireland relating to Malicious Injuries to Property' (24 & 25 Vict c 97) (1861).

'the inefficiency of the lighthouse service' has at least a tentative legal basis[65].

Almost since the emergence of economics as a distinct discipline, lighthouses provided a ready example of a public good, the sort of thing in which a mismatch of social and market value made government intervention necessary and beneficial. As John Stuart Mill explained,

> 'it is a proper office of government to build and maintain lighthouses, establish buoys, &c. for the security of navigation: for since it is impossible that the ships at sea which are benefited by a lighthouse, should be made to pay a toll on the occasion of its use, no one would build lighthouses from motives of personal interest, unless indemnified and rewarded from a compulsory levy made by the state.'[66]

Alongside lighthouses, Mill offered other examples: exploratory voyages for instance, or, more dubiously (though not unsurprisingly, coming from a former employee of the East India Company), the establishment of imperial colonies. Basic science, too − without state support, 'such researches could only be undertaken by the very few persons who, with an independent fortune, unite technical knowledge, laborious habits, and either great public spirit, or an ardent desire of scientific celebrity.'[67]

Nonetheless, it was lighthouses that became the public good of

---

[65] Episode 2.
[66] Mill, John Stuart, *Principles of Political Economy*, p589.
[67] Mill, *Principles of Political Economy*, p589.

choice in economics textbooks, the standard illustration of a benefit that would most logically be provided by government and not private enterprise. But, in 1974, British economist (and future Nobel laureate) Ronald Coase published a paper called 'The Lighthouse in Economics' attempting to refute that characterisation. Coase scrutinised the history of Trinity House, noting that, like Winstanley's Eddystone light, many early British lighthouses were privately built and owned; in exchange for the right to construct and run the light, the owner and Trinity House would split the subsequent fees, collected by agents from ships in port. 'The early history shows that, contrary to the belief of many economists, a lighthouse service can be provided by private enterprise,' Coase concluded. 'The role of the government was limited to the establishment and enforcement of property rights in the lighthouse.'[68]

Coase was trying to manoeuvre lighthouses into his own theoretical framework (laid out in his influential 1960 paper 'The Problem of Social Cost'), which was more sceptical of state control and regulation – 'there is no reason to suppose that government regulation is called for simply because the problem is not well handled by the market or the firm.'[69] Instead, Coase proposed, clear property rights and an open market would naturally lead to efficient outcomes. The notion of private enterprise producing public goods became ingrained in libertarian and pro-market economic circles. The Independent Institute, a California-based

---

[68] Coase, RH, 'The Lighthouse in Economics', *Journal of Law and Economics*, Vol 17, No 2, October 1974, p375.
[69] Coase, RH, 'The Problem of Social Cost', *Journal of Law and Economics*, vol 3, no 1, October 1960, p18.

libertarian think tank, even adopted a lighthouse as its logo in honour of Coase's paper, which, in their laissez-faire estimation, 'rescued the lighthouse as a symbol of courage, enlightenment and independence.'[70]

But, while Coase reproved other economists for using lighthouses to illustrate their ideology, they proved equally suspect in illustrating his own. The role of the government in running privately-owned lighthouses went well beyond the enforcement of property rights. The tolls which paid for the lighthouses were levied under state sanction and the threat of state penalty. A compulsory fee is not a voluntary, free-market transaction. As even sympathetic critics admitted, 'This distinction is perhaps the most important in all of political economy, and Coase fails to make it.'[71] The most enduring legacy of Coase's paper might be the cycles of critique and defence that it has attracted. Some fogs even a lighthouse cannot penetrate.

And, anyway, such abstractions, staking out positions on the continuum between 'public' and 'private,' obscure the peculiarly elemental nature of lighthouses and their purpose. Lighthouses – especially ones that warn against hazard, rather than simply guiding ships into port – tend to mark locales where circumstances can make questions of political economy suddenly seem very much beside the point. Palmerdale and his party might run in very different economic circles than the Fang Rock keepers, but the rocks – and the Rutan – put them all on equally perilous footing. At

---

[70] Independent Institute, 'The Lighthouse Logo'.
[71] Block, Walter, and William Barnett II, 'Coase and Bertrand on Lighthouses'. *Public Choice* vol 140, p2.

a place like Fang Rock, as one commentator has put it, 'if you're in a position to walk over to a captain to deliver your bill, he's most likely not in a position to pay you, because he's crashed.'[72]

3.

'There are good seamen dead because of you,' Harker fumes, scolding Lord Palmerdale. But Palmerdale's indifference is complete. His yacht might be wrecked, but the only thing on his mind is the deal, the information, the train waiting at Southampton, the London exchange, the windfall at the end of his journey. The Doctor asks after the rest of the crew – whether any other lifeboats might be in the water. Palmerdale has no idea. 'His Lordship,' Skinsale casually mentions, 'was in rather a hurry to leave the sinking ship.'[73] The working-class sailors are expendable.

How many sailors did Palmerdale leave to their fates? The name and registry of Palmerdale's yacht is unrecorded. What little we see of it suggests some similarity to other mid-size steam yachts of that gilded age: Hampshire squire Tankerville Chamberlayne's 104-foot *Amazon*, say, or the 127-foot *Aquilo*, built for William Phelps Eno, inventor of the stop sign. A later source recommended a 130-foot steam yacht carry a crew of 13 – for four or five passengers[74]. It would seem that as many as a dozen sailors lost their lives due to Palmerdale's rashness. Harker's fury is understandable: even before Palmerdale enters the Fang Rock lighthouse, he has already killed more people than the Rutan will.

---

[72] Davies, Daniel, 'Shine Your Light on Me...'
[73] Episode 2.
[74] 'Many Yachts to Go in Commission', *The American Marine Engineer,* vol X no 6, June 1915, p37.

Among the working class, sailors had more social mobility than many. Harker is about as high-ranking as an ordinary sailor can get. He is the yacht's coxswain, the vessel's chief petty officer; only the captain ranks higher. He has no small amount of professional skill. He is an expert helmsman. He knows Morse code, and how to operate a telegraph. But his position represents the apex of his possibilities. Perhaps that contributes to his acrimony: the closer one is to the ceiling, the more acutely one is aware of it. For all his ability, Harker remains trapped by his class, an attribute over which he has no control. One non-fictional sailor stated the dilemma plainly, imagining if one particularly ambitious Edwardian MP had instead been limited to Harker's possibilities: 'If Winston Churchill had been born in the house next door to the one I was born in and lived in there,' he noted, 'with a great deal of hard work he might have attained the lofty position' of a chief petty officer[75].

Churchill's career does hint at a possible background for Skinsale. A direct descendant of the Dukes of Marlborough, Churchill spent his childhood at Blenheim Palace, the family seat. But Churchill's uncle inherited the palace, while his father, Randolph Churchill, consistently lived beyond his means. Winston was forced to make a living as a journalist and a soldier. Palmerdale claims that Skinsale only 'acquired [his] taste for high living' after going into politics, but Skinsale retorts that he is 'an officer and a gentleman,' not some social-climbing upstart. One wonders if profligacy was a family trait.

The stain of dishonour Skinsale has brought upon himself is never fully explained. It is lucrative, to be sure; to cash in on the tip,

---

[75] McKee, Christopher, *Sober Men and True*, p13.

Palmerdale is willing to bribe Vince £50 on the spot, an enormous sum – with another £50 to follow. (£50 would have been approximately a year's salary for a new assistant lighthouse keeper; no wonder Vince is so conflicted[76].) In the script, Skinsale's indiscretion is simply referred to as 'information,' a vague catch-all. 'I gave you the information you wanted,' Skinsale tells Palmerdale[77]. Dicks' novelisation gets more specific: 'I gave you secret advance information about the Government's financial plans.'[78] But Skinsale himself leaves the most intriguing clue in introducing himself to the Doctor as 'the member for Thurley.'[79]

In actuality, Thurley (or Thurleigh, the spelling varies), a town of around 500 people just north of Bedford, was part of the constituency of Biggleswade, a district created in 1885. For its entire existence (until 1918, when constituency borders were again redrawn), the Biggleswade vote swung between the Liberal and Liberal Unionist parties, a distinction originally founded on the perennially vexing question of Ireland. The Liberal prime minister William Gladstone's promotion of Irish home rule split his party, with the Liberal Unionists officially forming in 1886. The Unionists' leader, Joseph Chamberlain, brought the party into coalition with the Conservatives, an arrangement that would persist through the Edwardian era. (The two parties eventually merged.)

---

[76] In 1906, a newly-hired assistant keeper received three shillings a day in wages, or around £54 a year. See *Minutes of Evidence Taken Before the Royal Commission on Lighthouse Administration*, p54.
[77] Episode 2.
[78] Dicks, *Doctor Who and the Horror of Fang Rock*, p62.
[79] Episode 2.

Chamberlain was an impulsive, charismatically demagogic figure who loomed over the political landscape. In 1895, the onetime radical Liberal became Secretary of State for the Colonies in Lord Salisbury's Conservative government, an ideal vantage for his imperialist outlook. But Chamberlain continued to thrust himself into other matters. By 1902, that included trade and, especially, tariffs. Winston Churchill recalled a dinner with a coterie of Conservative backbenchers, with Chamberlain as their guest. At evening's close, Chamberlain repaid hospitality with prophecy:

> 'I will give you a priceless secret. Tariffs! There are the politics of the future, and of the near future.'[80]

Tariffs were almost as divisive an issue as the Irish, with the divisions breaking largely along class lines: businessmen and landowners were mostly in favour of tariffs, while the working classes and the poor, more vulnerable to price increases, were mostly opposed. Free trade had been dogma throughout Victoria's reign. But, around the turn of the century, the increasing cost of building and maintaining the British Empire, combined with commercial threats from America and the continent, put tariffs back on the table. The expensive brutality of the Boer War, in particular, led the government to increase various taxes, including a small duty on imported corn. By the time the war ground to its conclusion in 1902, Chamberlain had begun to lobby hard for a so-called 'Imperial Preference,' a tariff regime that would exempt British colonies. However, the new Chancellor of the Exchequer, Charles Thomson Ritchie, was a free-trade diehard; while Chamberlain was on a post-war tour of South Africa, Ritchie rallied

---

[80] Churchill, Winston, *A Roving Commission: My Early Life,* p370.

the cabinet to his side. Chamberlain returned to find the corn tax repealed and momentum toward Imperial Preference seemingly stalled. In the spring of 1903, he went rogue, giving a blistering pro-tariff speech in his home base of Birmingham, putting himself in uncompromising opposition to free trade and the Conservative party that backstopped the coalition. Chamberlain had managed to split another party; the coalition was trounced in the 1906 elections.

Skinsale seems plugged into coalition politics, and to the tariff question: to Adelaide, he name-drops both Lord Salisbury, a Conservative Prime Minister, and, more interestingly, Bonar Law, whose real prominence still lay in the future (he would briefly serve as Prime Minister from 1922 to 1923), but who was in the thick of Chamberlain's tariff crusade as Parliamentary Secretary to the Board of Trade. The twists and turns of the tariff fight would have provided several inflections of government policy which could be leveraged in the commodities market – the corn tax, for instance. The honour Skinsale gambled away in Deauville may have been intelligence regarding the manoeuvring around tariffs, machinations that would test loyalties, pit rich against poor, and bring down a government.

But the fog and the rocks offer a chance to preserve the illusion of good character: if Palmerdale fails to cash in on Skinsale's tip, the breach of trust will be rendered inconsequential. So Skinsale smashes the wireless telegraph. In fact, Skinsale probably overestimated the risk to his privilege. In the summer of 1912, a number of ministers in Herbert Asquith's Liberal government were accused of buying shares in Marconi's company prior to public announcement of a contract with the firm to build a wireless network linking the whole of the British Empire – like Skinsale, exploiting their knowledge of government secrets. However, thanks to legal wiles and a partisan investigation, the only person to face consequences over the scandal was a journalist who published the allegations; he was found guilty of criminal libel and fined £100.

4.

As the Rutan begins to stalk the lighthouse's occupants and guests, the Doctor gets lost between Q and R. He is in the generator room, and has suddenly seized on the necessity of calculating the size of the alien attacker; Leela and Harker try to inform the Doctor of the more salient fact that Harker has seen Reuben (whose form, unbeknownst to the trio, has been taken over by the Rutan), but the information is momentarily lost in the Doctor's thicket of exposition ('in the space surrounding an electrically charged body there occurs an electric potential which is proportional to the charge Q, and inversely proportional to the distance R from the centre') before the Doctor brusquely snaps back to attention[81].

Coincidentally, Mr Ramsay in *To the Lighthouse* also gets lost between Q and R. In his imagination, he likens the work of philosophy to working one's way through the alphabet. At first, he regards his progress as salutary, if he does think so himself: '[H]is splendid mind had no sort of difficulty in running over those letters one by one, firmly and accurately, until it had reached, say, the letter Q. He reached Q. Very few people in the whole of England ever reach Q.' But he can't help skipping past self-congratulation

---

[81] Episode 3.

into darker regions of unrealised potential. 'What comes next? After Q there are a number of letters the last of which is scarcely visible to mortal eyes, but glimmers red in the distance. Z is only reached once by one man in a generation. Still, if he could reach R it would be something.'

But beyond Q lies doubt and despair:

> 'A shutter, like the leathern eyelid of a lizard, flickered over the intensity of his gaze and obscured the letter R. In that flash of darkness he heard people saying – he was a failure – that R was beyond him. He would never reach R.'[82]

The passage seems to be Woolf riffing on Leslie Stephen's philosophical efforts. Woolf's father was a well-known Victorian intellectual, and not just for his biographical efforts; a one-time Anglican minister, he renounced the cloth and became perhaps England's best-known agnostic. But the stall between Q and R echoes Stephen's contributions to the metaphysical debates of the day, in particular his essay 'What Is Materialism?,' first delivered as a lecture in 1886, and later published in his collection *An Agnostic's Apology*. Stephen regarded materialism – which held that matter was the fundamental basis of reality, that consciousness and thought were, in actuality, simply types of material interactions – as wanting. He dismissed the materialist notion that one could 'peep behind the curtain' of consciousness and perception to some more basic reality.

> 'The curtain is the reality. The effort to look behind it is an effort to get out of ourselves. It only plunges us into the

---

[82] Woolf, *To the Lighthouse*, pp33-34.

transcendental region of antinomies and cobwebs of the brain. The unknowable, which lies beyond, is not made into a reality by its capital letter.'[83]

The problem of materialism becomes a problem of how much we can know about what's outside – outside our perception, outside our consciousness, outside out experience. 'What are these mysterious entities, time and space, which define the nature of the material world?' Stephen wonders. 'Do we know of them as something existing altogether independently of ourselves, or are they made by our minds? and can we, if so, soar into transcendental regions altogether outside of them?' Those disinclined to such transcendentalism, he suggests, 'the ordinary mind, to which common-sense supplies the pole-star,' might well take comfort in an independent, materialist 'reality of sticks and stones'; but that gets us no closer to the relationship between thought and matter: 'in any case we cannot get outside our own consciousness.'

> 'When we speak of what happened when the solar system was still an incandescent mist, we are only extending our experience, as we do when we say that the fire is still burning in the room we have left. To say what would or did happen, outside of all experience, actual or potential – that is, supposing all experience to be annihilated – is to use words without meaning, as much as to say what I feel when

---

[83] Stephen, Leslie, *An Agnostic's Apology and Other Essays*, p144. Paul Tolliver Brown makes the connection between Mr Ramsay's alphabet and Leslie Stephen's essay in 'Relativity, Quantum Physics, and Consciousness in Virginia Woolf's *To the Lighthouse*', pp51-52.

I don't feel.'[84]

Trying to suss out the realities of what is going on at Fang Rock, the Doctor confronts the fallibility of his own experience of time and space. He is forced to acknowledge error, an error of inside and outside. 'Leela, I've made a terrible mistake. I thought I'd locked the enemy out,' he says. 'Instead, I've locked it in, with us.'[85] The Doctor shares Leslie Stephen's commitment to rationality – a commitment that Stephen would have elevates him above 'ordinary' minds – but, strangely, the Doctor's mistake is a product of excessive faith: faith in his own abilities and judgement. He has, perhaps, not paid attention to Woolf's main narrative concern: the stream of consciousness by which we get from point A to point B (or, for that matter, from point Q to point R). The Doctor's admission, a small but significant watershed, pinpoints a blind spot in the beacon of his logic. It is a believer's apology.

5.

To the Lighthouse does mirror **Doctor Who** in one unexpected way. The novel is also, after a fashion, a story of time travel, thanks to Woolf's interest in the biggest scientific celebrity of her own time: Albert Einstein, catapulted into fame on May 29, 1919, when observations of starlight bending around the gravity of the eclipsed sun confirmed his theory of relativity. To judge by the amount of her writing that seems to refer to and play off Einstein's theory, Woolf was fascinated by relativity – in particular, what it implied

---

[84] Stephen, *An Agnostic's Apology*, pp134, 135, 138-39.
[85] Episode 3.

about the multiplicity of experience and perception[86].

In Woolf's fiction – and *To the Lighthouse* is a paramount example – such multiplicity is often expressed, appropriately to Einstein's ideas, as a malleability of time. Sometimes it is the simple tug of present and past passing through a single consciousness. Near the end of the novel, James does finally travel to the lighthouse; he compares his adult impressions with his memory of how he saw the lighthouse as a child, when it was an oft-promised but seemingly unattainable destination:

> 'The Lighthouse was then a silvery, misty-looking tower with a yellow eye, that opened suddenly, and softly in the evening. Now –
>
> 'James looked at the Lighthouse. He could see the white-washed rocks; the tower, stark and straight; he could see that it was barred with black and white; he could see windows in it; he could even see washing spread on the rocks to dry. So that was the Lighthouse, was it?
>
> 'No, the other was also the Lighthouse. For nothing was simply one thing. The other Lighthouse was true too.'[87]

As James moves forward and back between present and past, the singularity of the material world dissolves, superseded by the fluid but manifest reality of perception. The conflict between James and

---

[86] Though my focus differs, much of my argument regarding Woolf and Einstein was sparked by Stockton, 'Public Space and Private Time: Perspective in *To the Lighthouse* and in Einstein's Special Theory', *Essays in Arts and Sciences* vol XXVII, pp95-115.

[87] Woolf, *To the Lighthouse*, p186.

his father is resolved in a triangulation of Einstein's theory, Leslie Stephen's repudiation of materialism, and the contrast between linear and holistic experiences of time.

But *To the Lighthouse* also engages with relativity on a more profound level, casting human interaction as an analogue of Einstein's interplay of light, mass, and perception. The centrepiece of the novel's first part is a dinner, arranged by Mrs Ramsay, and including, among the Ramsay family, all the guests on the island: Lily Briscoe; William Bankes, the reserved widower, wishing he were elsewhere taking refuge in work; Paul Rayley and Minta Doyle, who have themselves just become engaged; the caustic Charles Tansley. The meal starts off fractious. Mr Ramsay is out of sorts; Lily is lost in thought; Paul and Minta arrive late; Charles's burning surliness is in evidence. In Mrs Ramsay's mind, 'Nothing seemed to have merged. They all sat separate. And the whole of the effort of merging and flowing and creating rested on her.'[88]

And, indeed, Mrs Ramsay brings order to the system: the gravity of her personality, her attention, her measure of each guest, bends the evening's scattered light into social focus. Time seems to slow, until – as Mrs Ramsay serves William Bankes another slice of boeuf en daube – it practically stops:

> 'It partook, she felt, carefully helping Mr Bankes to a specially tender piece, of eternity... there is a coherence in things, a stability; something, she meant, is immune from change, and shines out (she glanced at the window with its ripple of reflected lights) in the face of the flowing, the

---

[88] Woolf, *To the Lighthouse*, p83.

fleeting, the spectral, like a ruby...'[89]

But the coherence is itself fleeting. The colour of that gem, the ruby, gives it away: a red-shift of the light as the sense of stability accelerates away from the observer.

It sets the table for what might be the novel's most relativistic experiment: 'Time Passes,' the interlude between the narrative's two main sections, an epic interstice. Woolf abruptly shifts from a leisurely exploration of the minutiae of human experience and emotion to an almost breathtakingly impersonal sweep of time. The perspective becomes that of the sea, and the lighthouse, a vantage from which the years accumulate and advance with little variation. Most audaciously, the deaths of three of the Ramsays – Andrew, killed in the war; Prue, dead in childbirth; and, most crucially, the sudden passing of Mrs Ramsay – are presented in the most offhand manner, with perfunctory glimpses set off from the narrative by brackets:

> '[Mr Ramsay, stumbling along a passage one dark morning, stretched his arms out, but Mrs Ramsay having died rather suddenly the night before, his arms, though stretched out, remained empty.]'[90]

Only the slowly decaying house and the omnipresent elements seem to remain: waves and seasons, erosion and entropy, cycles of storm and darkness, such that even human identity seems to lose its distinctiveness, becoming simply another tiny, contingent, not terribly important grain of noise in the transmission of the

---

[89] Woolf, *To the Lighthouse*, p105.
[90] Woolf, *To the Lighthouse*, p128.

universe. 'Not only was furniture confounded; there was scarcely anything left of body or mind by which one could say, "This is he" or "This is she."'[91] The temporary order of a house, a family, an era fades:

> 'The place was gone to rack and ruin. Only the Lighthouse beam entered the rooms for a moment, sent its sudden stare over bed and wall in the darkness of winter, looked with equanimity at the thistle and the swallow, the rat and the straw. Nothing now withstood them; nothing said no to them.'[92]

The acceleration through time plainly reveals the anxiety that haunts the rest of the novel, the anxiety that – to quote an aphorism often, though questionably, credited to the Edwardian Prime Minister Arthur Balfour – 'Nothing matters very much and very few things matter at all.' And it is very much an anxiety of class. Note how, in the 'Time Passes' section, the character focus shifts almost completely to the working class, to the Ramsay's servants, Mrs McNab and Mrs Bast. For the Ramsays everything is in flux; Mrs McNab and Mrs Bast provide the frame of reference in which change is minimised and the totality of the system – in this, case, the house – remains constant. 'Slowly and painfully, with broom and pail, mopping, scouring, Mrs McNab, Mrs Bast, stayed the corruption and the rot; rescued from the pool of Time that was fast closing over them now a basin, now a cupboard...'[93]

Those most invested in societal order would be most likely to

---

[91] Woolf, *To the Lighthouse*, p126.
[92] Woolf, *To the Lighthouse*, p138.
[93] Woolf, *To the Lighthouse*, p139.

notice when that order starts to slip; and the Ramsays, occupying a respectable upper-middle-class perch but (or thus) sensitive to how precarious that perch can be, feel it keenly. (William Bankes reflects that the Ramsays, despite their status, are not rich: 'Eight children! To feed eight children on philosophy!'[94]) As one scholar has put it: 'Cosmic indifference, with its counterpart of human instability, provides the ground for most of the action of the novel… The play of chance, the blindness of fertility – of growth without form, of change without purpose – the constant running down of whatever order has been established – all of this is what the characters confront at their moments of isolated awareness.'[95]

This sort of great-height view of human affairs briefly flickers across the Doctor's tête-à-tête with the Rutan scout:

DOCTOR

Why invade an obscure planet like Earth? It's of no value to you.

RUTAN

The planet is obscure, but its strategic position is sound. We shall use it as a launch point for our final assault on the Sontaran rabble.

DOCTOR

But if you set up a power base here, the Sontarans will bombard it with photonic missiles.

---

[94] Woolf, *To the Lighthouse*, p22.
[95] Price, Martin, *Forms of Life: Character and Moral Imagination in the Novel*, p324.

RUTAN

That is unimportant. It will serve the cause of our final glorious victory.

DOCTOR

And what about its people?

RUTAN

Primitive bipeds of no value. We scouted all the planets of this solar system. Only this one suits our purpose.[96]

The contrast in morality here is not between brutality and compassion, but between utility and harmlessness. Both the Rutan and the Doctor characterise humanity as insignificant. For the Rutan, that is reason enough to eradicate humans; for the Doctor, that is reason enough to let them be. But their perception of humanity comes from the same broad, galactic perspective. They speak as equals. They are, in a sense, from the same class, at least in comparison with the earthbound creatures they consider. To put it in Edwardian terms, that the Rutan's impulse is toward colonial exploitation and the Doctor's toward noblesse oblige doesn't change the fact that both regard human civilisation in a way reminiscent of aristocratic remove.

Part of the Doctor's remove results from travel through space: the Earth is but one planet, one pattern of evolution, one culture among millions. (As he chides Skinsale: 'You think your little speck in the galaxy's the only one with intelligent life?'[97]) But it also is a

---

[96] Episode 4.
[97] Episode 3.

consequence of the Doctor's relationship with time. His own timeline is so long, his engagement with other timelines so fluid and pliable, that normally directional chronology and causality instead become something more like three- or four-dimensional objects, turned and regarded from multiple angles. The Doctor's view of humanity – and his class-like distinction from it – flow from his relativistic experience of existence.

In that light, rather than the cerebral but limited Mr Ramsay, a better comparison for the Doctor is the eponymous protagonist of Woolf's 1928 novel *Orlando: A Biography*, who starts out as a boy in the age of Elizabeth I, and ends as a woman in contemporary, interwar England, having barely aged in the intervening 400 years. Like the Doctor, Orlando is a character who changes appearance, style, even gender across a superhuman lifespan, but whose identity remains anchored in a higher-level experience of time:

> 'It would be no exaggeration to say that he would go out after breakfast a man of thirty and come home to dinner a man of fifty-five at least. Some weeks added a century to his age, others no more than three seconds at most... Life seemed to him of prodigious length. Yet even so, it went like a flash.'[98]

Orlando is an aristocrat. Upon being transformed into a woman, she is taken in by an itinerant Romani caravan; though she is accepted, and even gains some measure of class-consciousness ('To the gipsy whose ancestors had built the Pyramids centuries before Christ was born, the genealogy of Howards and

---

[98] Woolf, Virginia, *Orlando: A Biography*, pp99-100.

Plantagenets was no better and no worse than that of the Smiths and Joneses'[99]), Orlando ultimately leaves the group. As with the Doctor, she can be among other people, she can observe and understand them, she can even empathise with them, but she remains forever and fundamentally apart[100].

6.

Throughout his visit to Fang Rock, the Doctor, as aristocrats are wont to do, disregards social convention and etiquette. The Doctor is not the only time traveller to consider such mores as blips in the temporal stream. Bertram Ingledew, a grey-suited, unflappable man who mysteriously arrives in Surrey in Grant Allen's 1895 novel *The British Barbarians*, is similarly dismissive of what he calls the 'taboos' of late-Victorian England. Ingledew assures Philip Christy, a nonplussed Englishman, that 'England has always been regarded with the greatest interest as the home and centre of the highest and most evolved taboo development.'[101] The visitor addresses everyone, men and women, high and low, with the same disarming

---

[99] Woolf, *Orlando*, pp147-48. Urmila Seshagiri has noted the undercurrent of racial and imperial anxiety in Orlando's departure, the fear that remaining with the caravan would be a sacrifice of her essential Englishness: see Seshagiri, *Race and the Modernist Imagination*, pp183-85.

[100] It is interesting to compare another interpretation of Orlando, in Alan Moore and Kevin O'Neill's comic book series **The League of Extraordinary Gentlemen**; like the Doctor, this Orlando, an actual immortal, has experienced a life of peripatetic adventure, but, unlike the Doctor, the resulting lofty perspective has dulled, rather than sharpened, the character's sense of morality.

[101] Allen, Grant, *The British Barbarians*, p42.

frankness. He blithely trespasses on the property of a local squire. He and Christy's sister Frida fall in love; Ingledew convinces her to leave her husband for him. When the husband tries to kill Ingledew – shooting him in the chest, only to witness 'a faint blue flame [...] issue from the wound in Bertram's right side and rise lambent into the air' – Ingledew reveals the truth: 'I forgot with what manner of savage I had still to deal. And now I must go back once more to the place whence I came – to THE TWENTY-FIFTH CENTURY.'[102] Frida, liberated, takes the gun and walks away.

> '"I'm going to follow him," she answered solemnly, in a very cold voice, "where you have sent him. But alone by myself: not here, before you."'[103]

The Doctor, too, arrives out of nowhere, from another time, alternately amused and irritated by the strictures of English society. So, this incarnation of the Doctor refuses to engage that society on any sort of equal terms. At the outset of his turn as the Doctor, Tom Baker was told by producer Philip Hinchcliffe to play the role with 'Olympian detachment'[104]; in *Fang Rock*, Olympus reaches new heights of inaccessibility. Throughout, Baker expresses the Doctor's distinction from those around him by giving a masterclass in variations on an old acting trick: keeping focus on oneself by never looking at another actor. Baker is more subtle than that, but he consistently uses his eyes to control a scene, to centre it on his distinctive presence.

---

[102] Allen, *The British Barbarians*, pp193, 195.
[103] Allen, *The British Barbarians*, p202.
[104] Pixley, 'You Ain't Seen Nothing Yet', *Doctor Who Magazine* Special Edition #8, cover date September 2004, p13.

Compare it with Colin Douglas's performance as Reuben – Douglas will often deliver part of a line while looking away; but he is setting up emphases, giving himself the opportunity to punctuate a line, a phrase, a word by turning his eyes back to the other performer. Baker almost never looks at an actor while listening to their dialogue, and he is parsimonious with his eye contact even when he is doing the talking. There are entire scenes – the one in the wireless room with Leela and Reuben, for example – in which Baker remains almost exclusively fixed on the fourth wall. His direct gaze is reserved for when the Doctor needs something from another character: information, compliance, obedience. Douglas's eye contact is rhythmic and interactive; Baker's is transactional and sequestering.

The Doctor's are not the only eyes to figure prominently in the story. *Horror of Fang Rock*, famously, turned Leela's brown eyes blue – the result, it is explained, of her gazing at the beam of the Doctor's amplified carbon oscillator.

LEELA

I'm blind. Slay me now. It is the fate of the old and crippled.

DOCTOR

You're neither old nor crippled. The effects of the flash will pass.

LEELA

You are sure?

DOCTOR

Hmm – blink. That's interesting.

LEELA

What is?

DOCTOR

Pigmentation dispersal caused by the flash. Your eyes have changed colour.[105]

The change was not a narrative decision, but a practical one: it allowed the blue-eyed Louise Jameson to cast aside her uncomfortable coloured contact lenses. But it does, perhaps, prompt the viewer, at the very end of the story, to go back and pay attention to how Leela perceives the action.

Leela has her own counterpart among the Ramsays on the Isle of Skye in *To the Lighthouse*: Lily Briscoe, another outsider who, too, is characterised through her eyes.

> 'With her little Chinese eyes and her puckered-up face, she would never marry; one could not take her painting very seriously; she was an independent little creature, and Mrs Ramsay liked her for it...'[106]

On multiple occasions, Mrs Ramsay considers Lily's 'Chinese eyes.' Woolf often used racial difference to symbolise social exteriority. Still, within the confined and homogeneous community of *To the Lighthouse*, the description is jarring, especially given its accompaniment of diminutive adjectives and the repeated suggestion that such an appearance is a liability rather than an advantage. But there is evidence that the difference Woolf

---

[105] Episode 4.
[106] Woolf, *To the Lighthouse*, p17.

intended to illustrate in Lily's eyes was an artistic one, and that the comparison reflected poorly on the comfortable society from which Lily is set apart.

The descriptions of Lily's painting owe something to the analyses of Roger Fry, the Bloomsbury group's resident painter and art critic. The distinction that Fry made most often in talking about visual art, across ages and civilisations, was between conceptual and perceptual art, between the artist who thinks about how something **should** look and the one who actually sees how it **does** look. The seeming progress of Lily's art in *To the Lighthouse* is from conceptual to perceptual, coming to realise that 'there was all the difference in the world between [...] planning airily away from the canvas and actually taking her brush and making the first mark.'[107]

Lily's painting seems to arrive at a form reminiscent of Fry's characterisations of post-Impressionist art, the works of Cezanne, Matisse, Picasso, and the like, which Fry almost single-handedly elevated to artistic prominence in Britain and the United States.

> 'Now, these artists... do not seek to imitate form, but to create form; not to imitate life, but to find an equivalent for life. By that I mean that they wish to make images which by the clearness of their logical structure, and by their closely-knit unity of texture, shall appeal to our disinterested and contemplative imagination with something of the same vividness as the things of actual life appeal to our practical activities. In fact, they aim not at illusion but at reality.'[108]

---

[107] Woolf, *To the Lighthouse*, p157.
[108] Fry, Roger, *Vision and Design*, p157.

And, as an example:

> 'Matisse aims at convincing us of the reality of his forms by the continuity and flow of his rhythmic line, by the logic of his space relations, and, above all, by an entirely new use of colour. In this, as in his markedly rhythmic design, he approaches more than any other European to the ideals of Chinese art.'[109]

In Fry's racially essentialist judgement, it was Chinese and Japanese art that most fully and elegantly embodied the perceptual line. The classification of Lily's eyes might symbolise her artistic evolution, which parallels Fry's posited west-to-east direction. Her 'Chinese eyes and her puckered-up face' could almost be an acquired characteristic – Lily is ever squinting after clarity, trying to see form and shape behind surface appearances[110].

Leela, too, is unusually perceptive. It is a common enough trope in the characterisation of 'primitive' characters: in the absence of more 'civilised' societal institutions and technology, they rely on their well-cultivated senses to survive. Signalling this persona with artificially-darkened eyes (and skin) certainly echoes the more problematic aspects of Lily's Chinese eyes, but, at least at the outset, Leela's character displayed a textured combination of instinct and intelligence particular to her background[111]. Perhaps

---

[109] Fry, *Vision and Design*, p158.

[110] For a discerning discussion of Woolf's use of Fry's theories and of racial differences in general, see Seshagiri, *Race and the Modernist Imagination*, pp150-67.

[111] Thomas Rodebaugh has analysed the implicit biases that could have informed Leela's eye colour in his **Black Archive** examination

ironically, it is in *Horror of Fang Rock* that the richer implications of her tribal, warrior background start to be pared down to mere heightened sensation. Nevertheless, she remains more attuned than the others to the things of actual life:

LEELA

Doctor, it's getting cold again.

DOCTOR

Are you sure?

LEELA

Yes. Last time it came like this, like a cold wave.

DOCTOR

I believe you're right.

SKINSALE

I don't feel anything.

DOCTOR

Leela's senses are particularly acute, and if she says it's getting colder, it's getting colder.[112]

But both Lily and Leela apprehend more than just line and weather. They are observers of people, of their interactions, of their ability (or lack thereof) to deal with life. That is to say: they are observers of class. And both women see past class to a reality beyond the

---

of *The Face of Evil*; see Rodebaugh, Thomas, *The Black Archive #27: The Face of Evil*, Chapter 4.

[112] Episode 2.

strictures of Victorian and Edwardian custom.

Lily Briscoe's rebuke to social expectation is subtle. After seeing Lily take a stroll with William Bankes, a widower and old friend of Mr Ramsay, Mrs Ramsay decides that, Chinese eyes or not, Lily might marry after all, and her matchmaking engine shifts into gear. However, though a friendship does take root between the two, marriage does not. For all his intelligence and solicitude, Mr Bankes is a creature of his time and place, and Lily, it is implied, intuitively resists such conformity. After Mrs Ramsay's death, Lily recalls a walk to the beach, long ago,

> '...she walking behind with William Bankes, and there was Minta in front of them with a hole in her stocking. How that little round hole of pink heel seemed to flaunt itself before them! How William Bankes deplored it, without, so far as she could remember, saying anything about it! It meant to him the annihilation of womanhood, and dirt and disorder, and servants leaving and beds not made at mid-day[...]'[113]

Lily comes to trust her own ideas of womanhood, and elude the conventional expectation of marriage.

> 'She had only escaped by the skin of her teeth though, she thought. She had been looking at the table-cloth, and it had flashed upon her that she would move the tree to the middle, and need never marry anybody, and she had felt an enormous exultation.'[114]

She makes her escape by looking. Lily turns her Chinese eyes into

---

[113] Woolf, *To the Lighthouse*, p172.
[114] Woolf, *To the Lighthouse*, p176.

an asset, a means to visualise her freedom from the limits of class.

Leela also takes a hard look at Edwardian class constraints. In fact, she practically stares through them: her frame of reference, her more practical outlook, minimises class. Even when she does create hierarchies, they are on practical lines: when she thinks their adversary might be another Time Lord, she hard-nosedly cancels out the Doctor's advantage ('there is nothing we can do'); when she is assured that the enemy is not Gallifreyan, victory is a logical certainty ('we have nothing to worry about')[115]. For Leela, the masquerade of English class divisions is a pointless distraction from the universal task of survival[116].

This is not the case with the only other woman in the lighthouse. Adelaide is not upper-class. She has, presumably, taken classes in typing and shorthand in order to find a job – a rather common path for unmarried working-class women in Victorian and Edwardian England. As another fictional secretary put it:

> 'I did not then know that every girl in London can write shorthand, and that typewriting as an accomplishment is as diffused as the piano; else I might have turned my hand to some honest trade instead, such as millinery or cake-making. However, a typewriter I was, and a typewriter must remain.'[117]

---

[115] Episode 4.
[116] Leela has already become acquainted with a few of the absurdities of Victorian class expectations in *The Talons of Weng-Chiang* (1977).
[117] Allen, Grant, *The Type-Writer Girl*, p15.

So laments Juliet Appleton, protagonist of *The Type-Writer Girl*, published in 1897 under the name of one Olive Pratt Rayner, but later revealed to be the work of Grant Allen, author of *The British Barbarians.* In both novels, unvarnished realisations of the hierarchy of class lead to female empowerment, of a sort. Juliet's takes the form of female solidarity. Though in love with her employer, she convinces him to instead return to his fiancée – sisters before misters.

Adelaide has no such epiphany. Her relationship with Palmerdale beyond her employment is left vague – though BBC Enterprises marketing materials, pitching the episode to overseas buyers, did put scare-quotes around 'secretary'[118] – but she aspires to class mobility, and that means total buy-in to Edwardian ideals of womanhood. At first, her gentility is not unappealing: when she arrives at the lighthouse, her courtesy toward Vince contrasts with Palmerdale's bullying. But her brittle sense of propriety forestalls any female cooperation. She considers Leela 'perfectly grotesque'[119]. She judges the Doctor's manners to be 'quite insufferable'[120]. Such pointed demureness becomes a liability. Confronted with the perilousness of the situation, she shows neither Frida's resolve nor Juliet's resilient self-awareness. Instead, she screams. At which point, in the story's most startling collapse of social hierarchy, Leela slaps her across the face.

---

[118] The marketing flier in question is reproduced in 'Production', *In-Vision* #24, p6.
[119] Episode 2.
[120] Episode 3.

7.

In the 'Time Passes' section of *To the Lighthouse*, Woolf described the last spring before the outbreak of the First World War:

> '[I]t was impossible [...] to resist the extraordinary stimulus to range hither and thither in search of some absolute good, some crystal of intensity, remote from the known pleasures and familiar virtues, something alien to the processes of domestic life, single, hard, bright, like a diamond in the sand, which would render the possessor secure.'[121]

In *Fang Rock*, it is, indeed, a diamond that renders the earth secure. It represents one last dissection of class and privilege in the tale, this time with the scalpel cutting both ways. For the Doctor, Palmerdale's diamonds are providential chunks of useful chemistry, the missing part in the weapon with which he hopes to destroy the Rutan mothership; the gems not suited to his engineering purpose he throws away. On this planet, though, diamonds are treasure. Palmerdale carries them as safeguards, talismans of fortune and rank. Human beings kill for diamonds, and die for them. Skinsale does – his tarrying to retrieve the diamonds the Doctor casts to the floor proves his undoing: a Rutan tentacle grabs and electrocutes the tardy victim.

Humanity's fate comes down to an object so expensive that most of humanity cannot afford one. The question lingers: is a democratic benefit (the lighthouse) hijacked and weaponised by the trappings of upper-class wealth (Palmerdale's diamonds)? Or are Palmerdale's tainted diamonds redeemed by their

---

[121] Woolf, *To the Lighthouse*, p132.

transformation, via the lighthouse, into instruments of salvation?

Because, often, all it takes to change an item's class is time. To give just one example: Virginia Woolf did visit the Godrevy lighthouse, twice, in 1892 and 1894. On the former occasion, the 12-year-old future novelist signed her name in her own hand ('Virginia Stephen') in the visitors' book. Thus did a utilitarian artefact become an object of privilege – in 2011, the Godrevy visitors' log was sold, at auction, for over £10,000[122].

---

[122] See Bonhams, 'Books, Maps, Manuscripts, and Historical Photographs, Including the Property of the Late Michael Silverman'.

PART 3: KNOWLEDGE AND TERROR

'The means whereby to identify dead forms is Mathematical Law. The means whereby to understand living forms is Analogy. By these means we are enabled to distinguish polarity and periodicity in the world.'

[Oswald Spengler, *The Decline of the West* (1918)][123]

1.

Unlike James Ramsay, Henry Wadsworth Longfellow never visited the lighthouse of his boyhood visions. From the upper floors of the family home on Congress Street in Portland, Maine, young Longfellow could see the Portland Head Light: a squat, white stone column three-and-a-half miles to the southwest, built in 1791. The location, a chunk of rock overlooking Casco Bay, had strategic importance; during the Revolutionary War, as artillery was hauled from the recently-captured Fort Ticonderoga to Boston, a few cannon were diverted to Portland Point, the handful of soldiers there having been ordered:

> '...on discovery of a ship, to fire a gun on Portland Point as an alarm, and in case any number of small vessels, more than two, and large enough for armed vessels, to fire two guns at Spring Point, and in case they prove to be enemies to use your best endeavours to annoy them.'[124]

---

[123] Spengler, Oswald, *The Decline of the West: Form and Actuality*, p2.

[124] Edwards, George Thornton, *The Youthful Haunts of Longfellow*, p177.

In 1847, after taking up residence in the Cambridge, Massachusetts, mansion that had been George Washington's headquarters during the war's Boston campaign, Longfellow returned to Portland. He took a holiday at the Verandah, a new hotel that would help create Maine's reputation as a vacation playground for well-off New Englanders. During that sojourn, the poet did not visit the Portland Head Light, but he did see the 'Two Lights,' twin towers at the southern end of Cape Elizabeth. Longfellow climbed to the top of the western tower to take in the views.

Somehow, out of these idyllic ingredients – childhood memories, a leisurely summer getaway – Longfellow fashioned a scene of elemental disquiet: 'The Lighthouse,' published in 1849.

> 'The rocky ledge runs far into the sea,
> And on its outer point, some miles away,
> The Lighthouse lifts its massive masonry,
> A pillar of fire by night, of cloud by day.'

The poem seems to elude Longfellow's every attempt to shoehorn it into a more conventional atmosphere or moral. Images of majestic ships and reassured sailors are inundated with unsettled language. The light's 'sudden radiance' carries a 'strange, unearthly splendour in the glare'; The tower becomes 'a dim, gigantic shape, / Holding its lantern o'er the restless surge.' The tides shout with 'speechless wrath, that rises and subsides / In the white lip and tremor of the face.'[125] (Even Longfellow's benign characterisations

---

[125] Longfellow, Henry Wadsworth, 'The Lighthouse', in *The Seaside and the Fireside*, pp41-44.

unwittingly hint at more dreadful images, as when he compares the lighthouse to 'the great giant Christopher,' unaware that early Christian legends, drawing on Eastern Orthodox sources, portrayed Saint Christopher as one of a race of dog-headed monsters that ate human flesh[126].)

The light consumes: the mariners' 'eager faces, as the light unveils, / Gaze at the tower, and vanish while they gaze.' And the light destroys:

> 'The sea-bird wheeling round it, with the din
> Of wings and winds and solitary cries,
> Blinded and maddened by the light within,
> Dashes himself against the glare, and dies.'

'A new Prometheus,' Longfellow calls the lighthouse, 'chained upon the rock, / Still grasping in his hand the fire of Jove.'[127]

Longfellow's wasn't the only new Prometheus introduced into 19th-century literature. Mary Shelley's *Frankenstein: Or, the Modern Prometheus*, published in 1818, mixed speculative science and Gothic horror into tropes which would shape much subsequent fantasy storytelling (including the Philip Hinchcliffe-produced run of **Doctor Who** immediately preceding *Horror of Fang Rock*). But it's the mythical allusion that concerns us here. *Fang Rock* amplifies Longfellow's fire of Jove into Frankensteinian proportions; as with Shelley's doomed protagonist, the rational beacon summons forth

---

[126] See, for instance, Friedman, John Block, *The Monstrous Races in Medieval Art and Thought*, pp72-75.
[127] Longfellow, Henry Wadsworth, 'The Lighthouse', in *The Seaside and the Fireside*, pp41-44.

a hideous, deadly monster. One can't shake the nagging suspicion that Promethean fire, whether guiding ships or giving life, both illuminates and incinerates. Among the strains of horror and fantasy informing *Fang Rock*, it is a common theme: knowledge isn't all it's cracked up to be.

2.

> 'Remember, Leela, don't fire until you see the green of its tentacles.'[128]

If every other historical detail was erased from *Horror of Fang Rock*, one could still make a plausible guess at its Edwardian setting based solely on the Rutan's true face.

> 'Reuben's body began to glow and melt and change... The human form warped and twisted and finally disappeared. In its place was a glowing shapeless mass. The creature was resuming its natural form [...]
>
> 'In place of Reuben's form there was a huge, dimly glowing gelatinous mass, internal organs pulsing gently inside the semi-transparent body. Somewhere near the centre were huge many-faceted eyes, and a shapeless orifice that could have been a mouth.'[129]

The Edwardian era marked the coming of age of what HP Lovecraft called the 'weird tale,'[130] a strain of storytelling that pushed Gothic horror's taste for the uncanny into realms of obsessive fantasies

---

[128] Episode 4.
[129] Dicks, *Doctor Who and the Horror of Fang Rock*, pp105-06.
[130] Lovecraft, HP, *Supernatural Horror in Literature*, p12.

and atmospheric dread – the sort of stories that Lovecraft himself would raise to apotheosis. And the Rutan ticks off all the boxes for a weird-tale nightmare: it is slimy; it is shapeless; it is protean. It is vaguely cephalopodic. And it is green.

The weird tale arose in the wake of the modern development of two branches of science, both germane to the goings-on at Fang Rock: psychology and oceanography. In 1879, Wilhelm Wundt founded the first laboratory of experimental psychology at the University of Leipzig, training an entire generation of researchers to put thought, emotion, and reflex on a rational, scientific basis. Those of Wundt's students who ended up in the United States show how pervasive the new psychology became. Hugo Münsterberg joined the Harvard faculty, where he influenced his fellow professor William James and taught new cohorts of psychologists (including William Moulton Marston, the creator of Wonder Woman). Walter Dill Scott applied psychological insights to advertising and management before designing intelligence tests for draftees into the First World War. James McKeen Cattell brought psychology into the American academic mainstream, and then – after being fired from Columbia University for opposing the draft – founded the Psychological Corporation, marketing psychological tests to business and government. It was all very analytical and practical.

Lovecraft regarded the essence of horror as recording and channelling those sensations that remained outside the new psychology's limiting rationality:

> '[T]hough the area of the unknown has been steadily contracting for thousands of years, an infinite reservoir of

mystery still engulfs most of the outer cosmos, whilst a vast residuum of powerful inherited associations clings around all the objects and processes that were once mysterious, however well they may now be explained.'

No matter how deep the likes of Wundt and his disciples – or, for that matter, the likes of Sigmund Freud and Carl Jung – might plumb human desire and fear, the bottom would always remain out of reach:

'Children will always be afraid of the dark, and men with minds sensitive to hereditary impulse will always tremble at the thought of the hidden and fathomless worlds of strange life which may pulsate in the gulfs beyond the stars, or press hideously upon our own globe in unholy dimensions which only the dead and the moonstruck can glimpse.'[131]

One of Lovecraft's touchstones for the weird tale, Welsh author Arthur Machen, expressed similar contra-rationalist scepticism in his 1902 polemic *Hieroglyphics*. '[A]rt is always miraculous,' Machen insisted. 'In its origin, in its working, in its results it is beyond and above explanation, and the artist's unconsciousness is only one phase of its infinite mysteries.' Machen illustrated his point with a satirical psychological questionnaire:

'1. Explain, in rational terms, the "Quest of the Holy Graal". State whether in your opinion such a vessel ever existed, and if you think it did not, justify your pleasure in reading the account of the search for it.

---

[131] Lovecraft, *Supernatural Horror in Literature*, p14.

'2. Explain, logically, your delight in colour. State, in terms that Voltaire would have understood, the meaning of the phrase, "the beauty of line."

'3. What do you mean by the word "music"? Give the rational explanation of Bach's Fugues, showing them to be as (1) true as Biology and (2) useful as Applied Mechanics.'[132]

The Rutan might be a weird monster par excellence, but the judicious working-out of elements both biological and mechanical in *Horror of Fang Rock* makes the story itself an interloper in the weird tale's milieu. That was by design – and, in fact, if writer Terrance Dicks had had his way, the contrast would have been even more extreme. Dicks' original story suggestion (eventually recycled into the season 18 serial *State of Decay* (1980)) had the Doctor encountering not Rutans, but vampires. 'I loved the possibilities for juxtaposition,' Dicks later explained. '**Who** was science fiction – modern and technological. And you could put that against something spooky like vampires that were old-fashioned, Gothic, and based in the supernatural.'[133] But the BBC demurred, fearing such a story would upstage the network's upcoming (and expensive) television adaptation of *Dracula*[134]. Instead, Dicks created the gelatinous, amphibious Rutan, a creature more befitting Robert Holmes' requested lighthouse setting. (Dicks did attach a vestigial vampire fang to the lighthouse itself.)

---

[132] Machen, Arthur, *Hieroglyphics*, pp149-50.
[133] Dicks, 'The Script Mutations', p8.
[134] *Count Dracula*, starring Louis Jourdan in the title role, was first broadcast in December 1977, three months after *Fang Rock*.

Much of the 'strange life' Lovecraft considered essential to the weird tale manifested in decidedly maritime form. Humans had long assumed that the seas, because of their unfixed and restless nature, accommodated all manner of fantastic and unusual creatures. Pliny the Elder, in his *Naturalis Historia*, characterised the ocean as a kind of blender, recombining the heavenly origins of life. 'The seeds of all bodies' fall from the stars, he wrote, 'principally into the ocean, and, being mixed together [...] a variety of monstrous forms are in this way frequently produced.'[135]

The pattern – the freakish nature of ocean creatures as the exception proving the natural-philosophical rule – was repeated again and again. A particularly good example is to be found in the description of starfish in *A Philosophical Treatise on the Works of Nature*, a 1721 survey by the English botanist Richard Bradley:

> 'The Mouths of all this Kind are in the Centre of their Bodies; and I do not find any **Orifice** for the Discharge of Excrement, no more than for the Service of Generation. So odd a Creature as this is well worth the Contemplation of such curious Persons as live near the Sea, where every Day they have Subjects enow to employ their Curiosity, and improve their Understanding.'[136]

Like psychology, marine biology was institutionalised in the late 1800s – for instance in 1872, Henri de Lacaze-Duthiers founded the Station biologique de Roscoff on France's Brittany coast, the first laboratory devoted to investigating the copious denizens of the sea

---

[135] Pliny the Elder, *The Natural History of Pliny*, p17.
[136] Bradley, Richard, *A Philosophical Account of the Works of Nature*, p56.

– but that only seemed to reinforce oceanographic mysteries in the fantastic imagination:

> 'Before my eyes was a horrible monster, worthy of appearing in teratological legends. It was a squid of colossal size, eight meters in length.
>
> 'It rolled and turned back with extreme velocity in the direction of the Nautilus. It stared with its huge, fixed eyes, tinted grey-green. Its eight arms, or rather eight feet, implanted on its head, which earned these animals the name of cephalopods, were twice the length of its body and writhed like the hair of furies [...] The mouth of this monster, a horned beak like that of a parrot, opened and closed vertically. Its tongue, a horned substance, itself armed with several rows of sharp teeth, came out, shivering, from these veritable shears... Its varying colour, changing with extreme rapidity according to the irritation of the animal, passed successively from livid grey to reddish brown.'[137]

This, the famous creature from Jules Verne's *20,000 Leagues under the Sea* (1871), was a product, not a source, of the fascination with sea monsters. Verne's inspiration was an 1867 travelogue by a French naval officer named Frédéric Bouyer, who recorded the sights and anecdotes of a voyage to French Guiana and back. Early in the book, Bouyer, sailing past the Canary Islands, muses on why some ships flourish and some founder:

> 'There are predestined ships, before which the waves

---

[137] Verne, Jules, *Vingt Mille Lieues sous les Mers*, pp392-93 (translation mine).

subside and the storms recede. Ships are born under stars like men. Like them, they suffer happy or unhappy chances. One would sometimes be tempted to believe that those great bodies of wood and iron to which our existence is attached... have integrated into a great individuality. I dare not embark on this theory for fear of running aground on a paradox.'

The impending metaphysical pitfall is interrupted by a report of debris on the vessel's port side. Various crew members give their assessment:

'– It's a capsized canoe.
'– It's red, it looks like a dead horse.
'– It's a bundle of seagrass.
'– It's a barrel.
'– It's an animal, we see the legs.'

But Bouyer knows what he is dealing with:

'I recognised the Giant Octopus, whose disputed existence seemed relegated to the field of the fable. I was in the presence of one of those weird beings that the sea sometimes brings forth from its depths as if to challenge naturalists.'

Bouyer's curiosity went beyond mere observation. He was the representative of a colonial power, on his way to a colonial outpost. (A substantial section of his memoir describes, in the most racially and morally inflammatory terms, the story of D'Chimbo, an African immigrant and fugitive who terrorised Guiana with a crime spree, the better to justify the supposedly civilising goals of the French colonial project.) Fabulous or not, the beast was something to be seized: 'The opportunity was too unexpected and too beautiful not to tempt me.'[138] But the octopus eludes capture.

Verne, building up the revelation of his own 'poulpe', has his characters discuss Bouyer's sighting. Apart from spelling Bouyer's name wrong ('Bouguer'), Verne's treatment of the report is journalistic. He situates his incredible creature within the bounds of published, cited reality.

It is just this sort of feint at rational plausibility that the weird tale will reject. Author China Miéville, discussing this fictional vogue for cephalopodic monstrosity and the shift in its justification, correlates it with late-19th-century social and political collapse: the Franco-Prussian war, the Paris Commune, the realisation of the essential brutality of imperial ambition: 'It is the growing proximity of this total crisis – kata-culmination of modernity, ultimate rebuke to nostrums of bourgeois progress – that is expressed in the shift to the morally opaque tentacular and proto-Lovecraftian radical Weird.'[139]

Edwardian England, in retrospect, has been portrayed as a coda to the long Victorian era, a last, lost English idyll before the outbreak of the First World War. But it was a period of upheaval – consider the Boer War horrors, or the chaos left in the wake of the Irish question, or the gulf of inequality that would lead to parliamentary fights over the social safety net of Lloyd George and Churchill's 'People's Budget' of 1909. Experienced day to day, Edwardian times were hardly free of disintegration and uncertainty. The times

---

[138] Bouyer, *La Guyane Française*, pp19-21 (translation mine).
[139] Miéville, China, 'MR James and the Quantum Vampire', *Collapse IV*, May 2008, p111.

produced a strange mixture of nostalgia and tumult.

Perhaps that's why *Horror of Fang Rock* splits the difference between Verne and Lovecraft. The Rutan's presence and history is cogently spelled out, but its form and appearance, while vaguely mollusc-like, surpasses any earthy analogue for disconcerting strangeness. Skinsale is shocked and baffled: 'That's the most horrible thing I've ever seen. What the devil is it?'[140] The Doctor, of course, elucidates. The sequence might embody not just the Edwardian era, not just the late 19th century, but the modern condition as a whole – profound, pervasive disorientation matched with a deep desire for some higher intelligence to neatly explain it all.

3.

HP Lovecraft only used a lighthouse setting once. 'The White Ship', published in 1919, relates the first-person testimony of one Basil Elton, 'keeper of the North Point light that my father and grandfather kept before me.' The ships that sailed by the light in his grandfather's day were legion; now, 'there are so few that I sometimes feel strangely alone, as though I were the last man on our planet.' Elton has become attuned to 'the secret lore of the ocean':

> 'Blue, green, grey, white, or black; smooth, ruffled, or mountainous; that ocean is not silent […] At first it told to me only the plain little tales of calm beaches and near ports, but with the years it grew more friendly and spoke of other things; of things more strange and more distant in space and

---

[140] Episode 4.

in time. Sometimes at twilight the grey vapours of the horizon have parted to grant me glimpses of the ways beyond; and sometimes at night the deep waters of the sea have grown clear and phosphorescent, to grant me glimpses of the ways beneath.'

He then tells of the White Ship, appearing out of the south when the moon is full. One night he sees a man on the ship's deck, bearded and robed, a seagoing sage. The man beckons Elton aboard: 'I walked out over the waters to the White Ship on a bridge of moonbeams.'

The White Ship embarks on an allegorical cruise. First there is the Land of Zar, 'where dwell all the dreams and thoughts of beauty that come to men once and then are forgotten.' Then Thalarion, 'City of a Thousand Wonders,' home to all the mysteries that humankind has tried, and failed, to comprehend. Then Xura, land of 'Pleasures Unattained.' Elton is tempted to disembark at each place, but his guide dissuades him. None ever return from Zar, he says, and those who visit Thalarion become 'daemons and mad things that are no longer men.' Xura offers the strongest allure, but

> 'Suddenly a wind blowing from over the flowery meadows and leafy woods brought a scent at which I trembled. The wind grew stronger, and the air was filled with the lethal, charnel odour of plague-stricken towns and uncovered cemeteries.'

Finally, they arrive at Sona-Nyl, the Land of Fancy, where Elton goes ashore. It is a place where 'there is neither time nor space, neither suffering nor death; and there I dwelt for many aeons.' But, one day, 'the beckoning form of the celestial bird' awakens in Elton the desire to see Calthuria, the Land of Hope. His guide tries to dissuade him; Elton is determined. After sailing past the basalt columns that supposedly mark the border of Calthuria, the travellers instead find themselves helplessly drawn to 'a monstrous cataract, wherein the oceans of the world drop down to abysmal nothingness.' Elton's guide sobs at their folly – 'The gods are greater than men, and they have conquered' – as the blue-winged celestial bird circles overhead. Elton shuts his eyes in anticipation of the crash: 'Out of that crash came darkness, and I heard the shrieking of men and of things which were not men.'

Elton opens his eyes and finds himself back at the lighthouse, where no time seems to have passed. But the light itself has gone out, 'for the first time since my grandfather had assumed its care,' and a ship has run aground, breaking up on the rocks. The next day, Elton finds a Longfellow-esque victim:

> 'With the dawn I descended the tower and looked for wreckage upon the rocks, but what I found was only this: a strange dead bird whose hue was as of the azure sky, and a single shattered spar, of a whiteness greater than that of the wave-tips or of the mountain snow.'[141]

'The White Ship' was an early entry by Lovecraft in a series of writings concerning visits to lands accessible only through dreaming. In his later novella *The Dream-Quest of Unknown Kadath* (written 1929, published 1943), the most extensive of these tales, the protagonist, Raymond Carter (a sensitive, struggling author,

---

[141] All quotations from Lovecraft, HP, 'The White Ship', *The HP Lovecraft Archive.*

which is to say, an obvious stand-in for Lovecraft himself) has apparently heard Elton tell of his travels, and ends up visiting the same locales. The North Point lighthouse itself symbolises one of Lovecraft's favourite themes: the restless, reckless human thirst for forbidden knowledge. The light illuminates the White Ship, the vessel of Elton's curiosity; after Elton abandons the paradisaical Sona-Nyl for the lure and devastation of the unknown, the light is extinguished. ('And thereafter the ocean told me its secrets no more.') The lighthouse's dual roles – searchlight and omen – are encompassed[142].

Still, even taking into account the terror of falling off the edge of the world, such dreamy symbolism seems far away from the grimy, grim frights of *Horror of Fang Rock*. (This is not to say that *Fang Rock* is not without its own dream logic. The way the plot, at the serial's climax, bends and twists to justify the change in Louise Jameson's eye colour hints at an outside dimension leaving its mark on *Fang Rock*'s internal reality, not completely unlike the fragmentary wreckage at the end of 'The White Ship.') The Rutan's invasion of Fang Rock rather calls to mind another Lovecraft tale: 'The Colour Out of Space,' first published in the September 1927 edition of *Amazing Stories*.

---

[142] Even if Lovecraft never revisited a lighthouse setting, lighthouses' unique sort of isolation, suspended between civilisation and nature, has continued to attract inhuman, shapeshifting Lovecraftian horrors. Most notable might be Jeff VanderMeer's Southern Reach trilogy of novels – *Annihilation*, *Authority* and *Acceptance* (all 2014) – set in an uncanny, doppelgänger-filled 'Area X' inspired by Florida's St Marks Wildlife Refuge and its abandoned lighthouse.

The story is another reminiscence, this time of Ammi Pierce, the last remaining resident of the overgrown woods west of Arkham, the fictional city at the centre of Lovecraft's sprawling mythos. The woods are soon to be flooded for a new reservoir; a surveyor for the project grows curious about the location's haunted reputation (a common prelude to unexplained horrors in Lovecraft's work) and hears Pierce's memories of events almost 50 years earlier, in 1882, when a meteorite fell out of the sky and landed on Nahum Gardner's farm. Professors from Miskatonic University come out to take samples of the unusually soft, luminous rock, which, 'upon heating before the spectroscope [...] displayed shining bands unlike any known colours of the normal spectrum.' The meteorite, they discover, harbours strange, fragile globules: 'The colour, which resembled some of the bands in the meteor's strange spectrum, was almost impossible to describe; and it was only by analogy that they called it colour at all.' A thunderstorm then apparently disintegrates the rock overnight. 'The stone, magnetic as it had been, must have had some peculiar electrical property; for it had 'drawn the lightning', as Nahum said, with a singular persistence.'

Within weeks, the vegetation on Gardner's farm begins to show odd characteristics, first growing bountifully large but inedible, then showing more and more traces of the indescribable colour, before turning grey and brittle. Animals in the area begin to succumb: '[S]ometimes the whole body would be uncannily shrivelled or compressed, and atrocious collapses or disintegrations were common.' Gardner's wife and son go mad, and he locks them in the attic. The sparks of personality and consciousness drain out of each member of the family. His other two sons disappear on trips to a glowing well with an increasingly dreadful aura. Pierce visits the farm one last time, only to find Nahum Gardner disintegrating before his eyes, croaking that 'it come from some place whar things ain't as they is here' before crumbling to dust. Pierce returns with police and town officials; when the sickly glow closes in on them, they escape up the side of a hill, from which they witness the farm's final destruction.

> 'When they looked back toward the valley and the distant Gardner place at the bottom they saw a fearsome sight. All the farm was shining with the hideous unknown blend of colour; trees, buildings, and even such grass and herbage as had not been wholly changed to lethal grey brittleness... over all the rest reigned that riot of luminous amorphousness, that alien and undimensioned rainbow of cryptic poison from the well − seething, feeling, lapping, reaching, scintillating, straining, and malignly bubbling in its cosmic and unrecognisable chromaticism.

> 'Then without warning the hideous thing shot vertically up toward the sky like a rocket or meteor, leaving behind no trail and disappearing through a round and curiously regular hole in the clouds before any man could gasp or cry out.'[143]

The parallels with *Fang Rock* are numerous: the object falling out of the sky; the isolated locale; the parasitic, nebulous extraterrestrial, somewhere between creature and substance. Lovecraft's imagination was, it seems, haunted by Rutan-like creatures, invaders and shapeshifters that would steal one's appearance and

---

[143] All quotations from Lovecraft, HP, 'The Colour Out of Space', *The HP Lovecraft Archive*.

identity. Among the story ideas he jotted down in his notebooks were several echoing the *Fang Rock* narrative:

> 'Inhabitant of another world – face masked, perhaps with human skin or surgically alter'd human shape, but body alien beneath robes. Having reached earth, tries to mix with mankind. Hideous revelation.

> 'Dream of awaking in vast hall of strange architecture, with sheet-covered forms on slabs – in positions similar to one's own. Suggestions of disturbingly non-human outlines under sheets. One of the objects moves and throws off sheet – non-terrestrial being revealed. Sugg. that oneself is also such a being – mind has become transferred to body on other planet.

> 'Insects or other entities from space attack and penetrate a man's head and cause him to remember alien and exotic things – possible displacement of personality.'[144]

All these extraterrestrial terrors, on the one hand, channel some portion of Lovecraft's racial anxieties. Lovecraft was a thoroughgoing racist, readily disparaging anyone of African or otherwise non Anglo-Saxon descent as sub-human and savage. In some stories, the allegory is obvious – particularly notorious is 'The Horror at Red Hook,' which transmutes Lovecraft's disgust with the immigrant population of Brooklyn into an imagined subterranean hellscape lurking below the streets. Even Lovecraft's description of the above-ground residents seethes with revulsion. '[T]he evil spirit of darkness and squalor broods on amongst the mongrels in the old

---

[144] Lovecraft, HP, *Miscellaneous Writings*, pp100, 101, 103.

brick houses,' he writes[145].

In other works, though, Lovecraft's racial animus evolves into a general derogation of humanity itself: as Lovecraft put it, 'the fundamental premise that common human laws and interests and emotions have no validity or significance in the cosmos-at-large.'[146] It is in this mood that Lovecraft reimagines the deep-sea-inspired monsters of the 19th Century – 'the nonhuman,' as Lovecraft scholar Jed Mayer has written, 'vividly rendered in multifarious forms, which threaten to displace humanity from its self-proclaimed position of privilege.'[147]

The most famous of these is Cthulhu, the high priest of the Great Old Ones, beings who could 'could plunge from world to world through the sky,' but who, since human time immemorial, have lain in stone houses in the city of R'lyeh, sunk beneath the ocean. Cthulhu bears all the hallmarks of the cryptozoological weird: 'a monster of vaguely anthropoid outline, but with an octopus-like head whose face was a mass of feelers, a scaly, rubbery-looking body, prodigious claws on hind and fore feet, and long, narrow wings behind.' And it is at sea that humans encounter the thing, stumbling upon:

> 'a coast-line of mingled mud, ooze, and weedy Cyclopean masonry which can be nothing less than the tangible

---

[145] Lovecraft, HP, 'The Horror at Red Hook', *The HP Lovecraft Archive*.

[146] Lovecraft, HP, *Selected Letters: 1929-1931*, p244.

[147] Jed Mayer, 'Race, Species, and Others: HP Lovecraft and the Animal', in Sederholm, Carl H, and Jeffrey Andrew Weinstock, *The Age of Lovecraft*.

substance of earth's supreme terror – the nightmare corpse-city of R'lyeh [...]

'The odour arising from the newly opened depths was intolerable, and at length the quick-eared Hawkins thought he heard a nasty, slopping sound down there. Everyone listened, and everyone was listening still when It lumbered slobberingly into sight and gropingly squeezed Its gelatinous green immensity through the black doorway into the tainted outside air of that poison city of madness [...] The Thing of the idols, the green, sticky spawn of the stars, had awaked to claim his own.'

['The Call of Cthulhu' (1928)][148]

The Rutan, as disturbing as it is, may not boast Cthulhu's capacity to instil incomprehensible, existential horror. But, in its own green, gelatinous way, it reminds human beings that they are, on a cosmological scale, nothing more than, as it opines, 'primitive bipeds of no value.'[149]

One of the most important influences on Lovecraft's later work, taking hold right around the time of 'The Colour Out of Space,' was Oswald Spengler's historical study *The Decline of the West* (*Der Untergang des Abendlandes*), which first appeared in English in 1926. Spengler's thesis – that cultures and civilisations rise and fall in arcs analogous to individual, biological life cycles, and that European-centred Western civilisation was currently in its old age –

---

[148] Lovecraft, HP, 'The Call of Cthulhu', *The HP Lovecraft Archive.*
[149] Episode 4.

dovetailed neatly with Lovecraft's general pessimism and his perception of 20th-century life as hopelessly decadent. The biological aspect of Spengler's historiography was ambitious and all-encompassing. As he put it:

> 'The plant is something **cosmic**, and the animal is additionally **a microcosm in relation to a macrocosm**. When, and not until, the unit has thus separated itself from the All and can define its position with respect to the All, it becomes thereby a microcosm. Even the planets in their great cycles are in servitude, and it is only these tiny worlds that move freely relative to a great one which appears in their consciousness as their world-around (environment). Only through this individualism of the microcosm does that which the light offers to its eyes – our eyes – acquire meaning as 'body,' and even to planets we are from some inner motive reluctant to concede the property of bodiliness.'[150]

The fears Lovecraft expresses in 'The Colour Out of Space' are Spenglerian through and through: the animal regressing into plant, the microcosmic being overtaken by the cosmic, individual free will being consumed by and subsumed into the All. The Rutan's presence at Fang Rock also puts all these fears into play. Cosmic forces, both biological and political, may well overwhelm the comparatively tiny microcosm of human concerns. Human bodies are taken over; human autonomy is annihilated. The Rutan itself is only a small part of a larger, collective organism – 'We are a Rutan

---

[150] Spengler, *The Decline of the West: Perspectives of World-History*, p4. Emphases in the original.

scout,' it informs the Doctor. When the Doctor casually shrugs that 'when you've seen one Rutan, you've seen them all,' he is not just addressing the Rutan's appearance, but its lack of individual identity. In a way, Reuben's human persona is doubly obliterated.

Even the total-war footing the Rutan scout espouses is symptomatic of how far Rutan civilisation is in decline. The Rutan's declaration that the species is making 'a series of strategic withdrawals to selected strong points' is not just, as the Doctor puts it, 'the empty rhetoric of a defeated dictator,' but a sign of decaying Rutan culture, its very language infected by militarism and arrogance[151]. Lovecraft saw something of the same effect in his own era. 'Spengler is right, I feel, in classifying the present phase of western civilisation as a decadent one,' he wrote, 'for racial-cultural stamina shines more brightly in art, war, and prideful magnificence than in the arid intellectualism, engulfing commercialism, and pointless material luxury' of the 20th century[152].

Nevertheless, Lovecraft did think that Spengler took his biological framework too far:

> 'In effect, the parallel may indeed be close; for it is certain no civilisation can last more than a limited length of time without going thro' various typical phases of decline. But when one considers the nature of the interdependence betwixt the parts of an organick unit, and compares this type of indivisible unit and inevitable development with the

---

[151] Episode 4. In this, the characterisation of the Rutans matches that of their Sontaran enemies.
[152] Lovecraft, *Selected Letters: 1925-1929*, p228.

looser bonds linking the elements of a culture, it becomes plain that the case is one of **resemblance** rather than of identity.'[153]

It is at least an intriguing echo of Lovecraft's critique that the encounter at Fang Rock, the collision of human society and a dying Rutan civilisation, hinges on the gap between identity and resemblance.

4.

In the era surrounding *Fang Rock*, green was an unofficial colour of decadence. Writing about Thomas Wainewright, the 19th-century English artist widely suspected of having poisoned his uncle, sister-in-law, and mother-in-law, Oscar Wilde noted that the killer 'had that curious love of green, which in individuals is always the sign of a subtle artistic temperament, and in nations is said to denote a laxity, if not a decadence, of morals.'[154] Wilde himself adopted the colour by way of the artificially-dyed green carnation, which became a favourite emblem of the decadent set. When Robert Hichins anonymously published his novel *The Green Carnation* – a very-thinly disguised account of Wilde's romance with Lord Alfred 'Bosie' Douglas – enough people assumed that Wilde was the author that he was compelled to issue a denial: 'I invented that magnificent flower,' Wilde acknowledged, but he had not written the book[155]. Poet Richard Le Gallienne, who also had a brief affair with Wilde, grew suspicious of green, deciding there was

---

[153] Quoted in Joshi, ST, *HP Lovecraft: The Decline of the West*, p319. Emphasis in the original.
[154] Wilde, Oscar, 'Pen, Pencil, and Poison', in *Intentions*, p59.
[155] Ellmann, Richard, *Oscar Wilde*, p424.

'something not quite good, something almost sinister, about it – at least, in its more complex forms... [T]he green of the aesthete does not suggest innocence.'[156] (Indeed, *The Green Carnation* would be used against Wilde in the libel trial that destroyed his reputation.)

At the time, green was not yet the characteristic colour of monsters, literary or extraterrestrial. There had been hints – the grey-green eyes of Verne's squid, for example. Or maybe Sheridan Le Fanu's 'Green Tea' (1872), in which a clergyman's hallucinations of a demonic monkey are attributed by the doctor-narrator to excess consumption of the titular beverage, which has disturbed a certain fluid that courses through the nervous system 'that which we have in common with spirits'; the reverend's green-tea habit has exposed his nerves to direct communication from the spirit-world[157]. But the green Martians of Edgar Rice Burroughs' *A Princess of Mars* and the green slime that smothers the lair and form of Cthulhu lay in the future. By 1977, on the other hand, green aliens were a cliché, to *Fang Rock* writer Terrance Dicks' amusement. 'Green!' Dicks once chuckled. 'The colour of monsters is green. That seems to be a particular thing.'[158] In *Fang Rock*'s Edwardian-era reality, however, the Rutan is getting a jump on popular culture by showing up verdant.

Green is, of course, the colour of growth: healthy crops, summer foliage. Still, for all its connotations of vegetal bounty or Arcadian beauty, green does have a long association with disease and death.

---

[156] Le Gallienne, Richard, 'The Boom in Yellow', in *Prose Fancies (Second Series)*, p79.
[157] Le Fanu, J Sheridan, 'Green Tea', in *In a Glass Darkly*, vol I, p93.
[158] *Doctor Who: Thirty Years in the TARDIS* (1993).

Consider the book of *Revelation*, the sixth chapter, the eighth verse, as given in the 14th-century Wycliffe Bible:

> 'And lo! a pale hors; and the name was Deth to hym that sat on hym, and helle suede hym. And power was youun to hym on foure partis of the erthe, for to sle with swerd, and with hungur, and with deth, and with beestis of the erthe.'

The 'pale horse' that Death rides made it into the King James Version, and from there into nearly every subsequent English Bible translation. But the original Greek had a somewhat different steed: a 'híppos chlorós' or 'green horse'. (The New Standard Revised Version, published in 1989, finally gets it right: Death's mount is a 'pale green horse.') The Rutan somehow encompasses both strains of green: it is fecund in its fatality, a source of burgeoning death. As Alexander Theroux has written, green is 'the colour of more force and guises than are countable'[159].

Whether by happenstance or design, the pale, glowing green of the Rutan scout and the purplish-pink streak of light left by its ship are very close to being complementary colours, across from each other on the traditional colour wheel. The Rutan might be at the forefront of alien colouration, but the green-purple combination is a few decades behind the times. Complementary colours were a Victorian, not an Edwardian, vogue; for example, in *The Book of Household Management*, a sort of field manual for Victorian housewives written by the indispensable domestic authority Isabella Beeton and first published in 1861, Mrs Beeton offered this advice for choosing apparel:

---

[159] Theroux, Alexander, *The Secondary Colours: Three Essays*, p209.

'The colours which go best together are green with violet; gold-colour with dark crimson or lilac; pale blue with scarlet; pink with black or white; and grey with scarlet or pink.'[160]

Up-to-date Edwardians opted for paler colours, and were more likely to combine colours that were colour-wheel adjacent – green with yellow or blue, say.

Variations of the traditional colour wheel, based on the classification of red, yellow, and blue as the primary colours, had been in use since Isaac Newton first proposed it in his 1704 *Opticks*. Still, Newton had his naysayers – in particular, Johann Wolfgang von Goethe, whose own *Theory of Colours* (*Zur Farbenlehre*, published in 1810) criticised Newton's methods while expounding Goethe's own phenomenological and experiential ideas of colour. For Goethe, Newton's manipulations of light and prisms fatally lacked consideration of that most elementary instrument of colour detection: the eye. Examining and describing his own perceptions of colour, Goethe produced something more akin to psychology than physics. Philosophers were intrigued by Goethe's ideas, some artists experimented with palettes based on his framework, but the scientific community remained unconvinced. According to one reviewer (who happened to be John Tyndall, scientific advisor to Trinity House), Goethe 'is always rich in facts. But, when he comes to deal with physical theory, the poverty and confusion of his otherwise transcendent mind become conspicuous.'[161]

Toward the end of the 19th century, though, a portion of Goethe's

---

[160] Beeton, Isabella, *The Book of Household Management*, p5.
[161] Tyndall, 'Goethe's Farbenlehre (Theory of Colours)', *Popular Science Monthly*, vol XVII, no 19, July 1880, p314.

exposition was revived in a more scientifically rigorous way. Goethe had proposed a symmetrical colour wheel that had colours facing off which 'reciprocally evoke each other in the eye. Thus, yellow demands violet; orange, blue; purple, green; and vice versa...'[162] In the 1890s, a German physiologist named Ewald Hering formalised Goethe's colour demands into what came to be called opponent colour theory. Hering simplified Goethe's six colours into two irreconcilable pairs – red versus green, yellow versus blue – based on the fact that the human eye cannot register a colour that could be described as reddish-green, for instance. The perception of colour could be based on the perception of **differences**, between red and green, yellow and blue[163].

What makes all this relevant to the Doctor's presence on Fang Rock is that, in 1974, psychologists Richard Solomon and John Corbit extended Ewald's concept into a more generalised theory of behaviour. In place of colours, they charted opposing pairs of emotions: pleasure and pain, fear and relief. Mood and action are motivated by the differences between pairs. Solomon and Corbit proposed the theory as an explanation for addictive behaviours – drug addiction, say, but also thrill-seeking. They cited the example of skydivers:

> 'When parachutists make their first jump, they are often terrified, judging by telemetered autonomic responses and photographed facial expressions. When they land safely, they look stony-faced or stunned for several minutes, then gradually resume normal composure. After the parachutists

---

[162] Goethe, Johann Wolfgang von, *Goethe's Theory of Colours*, p21.
[163] See Hering, Ewald, *Outlines of a Theory of the Light Sense.*

have made several jumps and are experts, their responses are different. When jumping, they are no longer terrified. They may be anxious, tense, or even eager. After they land safely, they feel exuberant, exhilarated, and good. They like the feeling, and the mood lasts sometimes for hours. Such parachutists love to jump because of this after-feeling.'[164]

The Doctor shows bursts of seeming euphoria as the alien threat comes into focus, most notably, his inappropriately, irrepressibly cheerful invitation to Palmerdale, Skinsale, and Harker: 'This lighthouse is under attack, and by morning we might all be dead; anyone interested?' Solomon and Corbit might chalk such giddiness up to the Doctor's one-crisis-after-another career, seven centuries' worth of alternating fear and relief creating an irresistible urge to plunge into danger again and again. The Doctor gets his fix by entering an impossibly fraught situation and, well, fixing it. As we have noted before, the Doctor's arrival at Fang Rock just at the moment of greatest threat might be considered outrageously coincidental; but, again – and according to opponent theory – isn't such a place and time exactly where the Doctor would be expected to be found?

5.

Reuben, for one, expects **something** to be found at Fang Rock; at least, he is not surprised when something turns up. 'They always said the Beast of Fang Rock would be back,' he warns. The Doctor, who has spent hundreds of years finding logical explanations for

---

[164] Solomon, Richard L, and John D Corbit, 'An Opponent-Process Theory of Motivation: I. Temporal Dynamics of Affect', p123.

the preternatural, is not impressed.

LEELA

Do you think the Beast ate him?

DOCTOR

What beast?

LEELA

The Beast of Fang Rock.

DOCTOR

There's no such animal.

LEELA

But Reuben said there was.

DOCTOR

Leela, the people round here have been fisherfolk for generations. They're almost as primitive and as superstition-ridden as your lot are.[165]

The Flannan Isles — where the three lighthouse keepers disappeared in 1900, providing inspiration for Wilfred Wilson Gibson's poem, and, by extension, *Horror of Fang Rock* — has a history of triggering superstition. In 1695, a Scottish traveller named Martin Martin toured the islands off the western coast of Scotland, publishing his impressions a decade later. At the time, the Flannan Isles were, Martin reported, home to some 70 sheep;

---

[165] Episode 2.

but residents of the neighbouring Isle of Lewis would boat over to the Flannan Isles every summer to 'make a great purchase of fowls, eggs, down, feathers, and quills.' The visitors approached the Isles with an inventory of superstitious ritual:

'If any of their crew is a novice, and not versed in the customs of the place, he must be instructed perfectly in all the punctilioes observed here before landing [...] After their landing, they fasten the boat to the sides of a rock, and then fix a wooden ladder, by laying a stone at the foot of it, to prevent its falling into the sea; and when they are got up into the island, all of them uncover their heads, and make a turn sun-ways round, thanking God for their safety. The first injunction given after landing, is not to ease nature in that place where the boat lies, for that they reckon a crime of the highest nature, and of dangerous consequence to all their crew; for they have a great regard to that very piece of the rock upon which they first set their feet, after escaping the danger of the ocean.'

In addition:

'They must not so much as once name the islands in which they are fowling by the ordinary name Flannan, but only the country. There are several other things that must not be called by their common names, *e.g.*, Visk, which in the language of the natives signifies Water, they call Burn; a Rock, which in their language is Creg, must here be called Cruey, *i.e.* hard; Shore in their language, expressed by Claddach, must here be called Vah, *i.e.*, a Cave; Sour in their language is expressed Gort, but must here be called Gaire, *i.e.,* Sharp; Slippery, which is expressed Bog, must be called Soft; and several other things to this purpose.'

Martin asked one of the visitors 'if he prayed at home as often, and as fervently as he did when in the Flannan Islands, and he plainly confessed to me that he did not'[166].

Reuben's home prayer habits remain a mystery, but, after learning of Ben's death, he makes the sign of the cross – donning divine armour to combat the Beast, perhaps. His suspicions, though, more immediately settle on the Doctor and Leela. The fabled Beast is not even mentioned until the second episode. That didn't stop previews of *Horror of Fang Rock* from prominently advertising the supposed paranormal presence, as in *The Guardian*, for instance:

> 'He's back – Tom Baker as the Doc, Louise Jameson as sideperson Leela, and a synopsis that reads like something Ernie Wise wrote for Hammer: still in fin-de-siècle London, he wants to take her to Brighton, but the Tardis dumps them in dense fog on Fang Rock, remote lighthouse, where 80 years ago the Beast came, two men died, another went mad, and now... aaarrgh'[167]

The Observer similarly anticipated a serial marked by 'legendary beasts, nameless deaths and unhinged minds'[168].

The story sets the table for a clash between myth and rationality,

---

[166] Martin, Martin, *A Description of the Western Islands of Scotland, Circa 1695*, pp16-19.
[167] 'Weekend TV and Radio', *The Guardian*, 3 September 1977, p11.
[168] W Stephen Gilbert, 'The Week in View', *The Observer*, 28 August 1977, p27.

between **Doctor Who**'s allegiance to logical exposition – scientifically or technologically explicating even the most fantastic happenings – and Lovecraft's complex censure of modern science and technology, progress that has reached dangerously beyond human control or even comprehension. But the contest never comes. The Beast fades into the general background of unease, pushed aside by more pressing concerns. The monster that takes over Reuben's form is straightforward, even quotidian: a footsoldier, a functionary. *Horror of Fang Rock* is a battle of wits, not magic.

But the story still embodies the lighthouse's bifurcated symbolism of knowledge as both benefit and admonition. Even those trapped with the Doctor on Fang Rock who come to comprehend the exact nature of the threat they face still perish. All that is left is for their dead forms to be mathematically accounted for. It is as if Longfellow's sea-bird understood the inner workings of the lighthouse's glare, but still flew into the glass.

PART 4: FACT AND FICTION

'Make the tale live for us
In all its many bearings
O Muse'

[Homer, *Odyssey* (trans TE Lawrence)][169]

1.

They can't keep their story straight. One saw lights near Hell Point, but the other two did not. Arriving at the island, they were greeted by three black seals. Or was it three black birds? Or maybe three black cats, feral and wary. The chair beside the table was tipped over on its back; the chair was tipped over on its side. A cup was smashed on the table – or else it was smashed on the floor.

But all three heard the foghorn around Hell Point, where there should have been no foghorn. They all saw the horde of black rats scurrying over the transom of the lighthouse door, and over their feet. They all saw the open door, the oatcakes still on the table; but they found no sign of the lighthouse keepers.

And then, abruptly, the three officers of the ship sent to relieve the crew of the Fladda Isle lighthouse transform into the record of their own testimony, formal, fixed, bureaucratic. The court of inquiry has made its decision. 'Death by misadventure. An open verdict.' And with that, their story is delimited. Its narrative arc is set.

---

[169] Homer, *The Odyssey of Homer*, p. xxiii.

In the end, the lighthouse is automated. There are no more stories to tell; the people who would tell them are gone. All that are left are shadows.

2.

In September 1980, almost three years to the day after the first transmission of *Horror of Fang Rock*, Peter Maxwell Davies' one-act chamber opera *The Lighthouse* premiered in Edinburgh. The opera was inspired by the same event that inspired *Fang Rock* and, before that, the Wilfrid Wilson Gibson poem that the Doctor quotes at *Fang Rock*'s conclusion: the unsolved disappearance of three lighthouse keepers from the Flannan Isles lighthouse in 1900. For all their differences – in tone, in narrative strategy, in artistic objective – *The Lighthouse* and *Fang Rock* overlap in crucial ways. Both make use of the isolated, self-enclosed setting; both posit frightening, fantastic solutions to their Flannan-Isles-like mysteries; both hinge on a fatal rift between appearances and reality. (Davies attributed his inspiration to the mention of the Flannan Isles disappearance in Craig Mair's *A Star for Seamen* (1978), a history of the Stevenson family's lighthouse engineering efforts; given the timing, though, it is not completely outside the realm of possibility that *Horror of Fang Rock* also provided a spark.)

Despite their discrepancies as to lights, animals, and chairs, the explanation the three officers propose in *The Lighthouse* is, basically, the rational interpretation of the similar disappearance of the keepers of the Flannan Isles lighthouse: one keeper, as the officers sing, 'could have been called out urgently by another keeper to the aid of a third, in difficulties down at the jetty, and then they were all three swept away.'[170] Davies, a resident of the Orkney islands for the last four decades of his life, witnessed the sea's capacity for sudden force; the howl of the elements in *The Lighthouse* was captured by someone who knew the danger well. Davies has the theory sung by all three officers, in rhythmic unison and close harmony. The story conforms.

But that is hardly the end of the story. The court of inquiry, the testimony, verdict, and aftermath, forms the prologue of *The Lighthouse*, not the denouement. 'It was hard to find men to replace the three dead,' one officer sings, as the others accompany with quiet humming. 'The place now had a bad name.' A robotic light is installed, flashing to a jerky, nine-note motif. 'The lighthouse is now automatic,' the three sing, in the same bright, stiff, mechanical intervals. 'The lighthouse is dead dead dead dead dead.' And then the real story – or is it the 'real' story? – can begin.

Early reports of the disappearance of the keepers at the Flannan Isles lighthouse found the story curious, but readily explainable. 'DISASTER AT A LEWIS LIGHTHOUSE,' announced *The Scotsman* on December 28, 1900. 'THREE MEN DROWNED.'

> 'On the boat's crew landing at Eilean Mohr no one was to be seen. The tower and residences of the keepers was searched, but none of the men could be found. A rocket was fired, but there was no response, and the painful conviction was forced home that the lighthouse keepers had been swept off the island and drowned. All the clocks in the building were stopped, from which it is considered possible

---

[170] Davies, Peter Maxwell, *The Lighthouse: Vocal Score*, pp39-40.

that the disaster occurred about ten days ago – presumably on Thursday last, the 20th – the day of the terrific gale which did so much damage all over Scotland and wrecked part of the Shetland fishing fleet.'[171]

The circumstances surrounding the loss of the three keepers – James Ducat, the principal keeper; Thomas Marshall, the second assistant; and Donald McArthur, temporarily substituting for a sick colleague – were tragic but unsurprising. A storm blew up; the three keepers were caught out on the rocks; a large wave rose up suddenly and knocked the men into the sea.

But the incident at the Flannan Isles light became a magnet for all manner of 'real stories.' Take the question of the weather: after further investigation by the Northern Lighthouse Board, the probable date for the keepers' disappearance was pushed back from 20 December ('the day of the terrific gale') to 15 December. That was when the logbook stopped being updated; that night, a passing ship, the *Archtor*, noticed that the light was out. (This paradoxical detail – 'A lighthouse without a light,' as the Doctor puts it – made its way into both *Fang Rock* and Wilfrid Wilson Gibson's poem[172].) The *Archtor* reported the conditions as 'clear, but stormy,' but the idea took hold that the men perished when the seas were calm. As early as 1929, there appeared what purported to be excerpts from the Flannan Isles logbook hinting that some sort of nervous dread, rather than inclement weather,

---

[171] This and other contemporary reports on the disappearance have been compiled in Dash, Mike, 'The Vanishing Lighthousemen of Eilean Mòr', *Fortean Studies*, vol 4.
[172] Episode 1.

might have claimed the men:

'Dec. 12: Gale, north by north-west. Sea lashed to fury.

'Stormbound 9pm. Never seen such a storm. Everything shipshape. Ducat irritable.

'12pm. Storm still raging. Wind steady. Stormbound. Cannot go out. Ship passed sounding foghorn. Could see lights of cabins. Ducat quiet. McArthur crying.

'Dec. 13: Storm continued through night. Wind shifted west by north. Ducat quiet. McArthur praying.

'12 noon. Grey daylight. Me, Ducat, and McArthur prayed.

'Dec. 15: 1pm. Storm ended. Sea calm. God is over all.'[173]

That this material appeared in a short-lived pulp magazine called *True Strange Stories* should give some indication of its historical veracity. Nevertheless, the supposed calm of that day's weather continued to raise the occasional eyebrow. John Michell's, for instance:

'How the three men could disappear from the Flannan Isles on a calm day is a question which has never been answered. In a case like this where there appears to be no natural solution, it was only to be expected that people should look for a more sinister cause for the tragedy.'[174]

Michell, then on the cusp of a career as one of Britain's most

---

[173] Fallon, Ernest, 'The Strange Log of the Seven Hunters', quoted in Dash, Mike, 'True Strange Stories?' *Fortean Times* #352, p41.
[174] Michell, John, *The Flying Saucer Vision*, p115.

contrarian esotericists, located that cause in a supposed race of supernatural 'little men' living in the western Scottish isles, especially Eilean Mòr, to which the primitive locals had offered oblation.

> 'In light of what we can deduce of the ways of worship and sacrifice of the past, the disappearance of the Flannan Island lighthouse keepers may be seen as an extraordinary repetition of an ancient sacrificial ceremony. The men were taken from the Long Island near Callernish and ferried over to the island of the dead, Eilean Mòr, where they were installed in a tower, similar to those once used for human sacrifice... In the same way as a magic ritual, if properly carried out, may have a predictable result, the sequence of events involved in taking the lighthouse keepers to the Flannan Islands tower ended in their disappearance. The ritual of human sacrifice to the little gods of the western islands was re-enacted, and had the same consequences for the victims as in the days when the great temple of Callernish saw human offerings dispatched to the island of the gods many centuries earlier.'[175]

This notion circled back to Michell's main argument, that the seeming alignment of various natural landmarks and mystical locations and structures across the landscape were, in fact, 'ley lines,' navigational markers for extraterrestrials. The 'little men' who took in tribute the lives of the Flannan Isles keepers, Michell concluded, were probably not of this earth.

---

[175] Michell, *The Flying Saucer Vision*, pp117-18.

3.

In debating the believability of an alien presence on Fang Rock, both Skinsale and the Doctor place it in the context of storytelling – and one storyteller in particular:

DOCTOR

I've never been more serious, Colonel. We are facing an enemy of greater power than you can dream of.

SKINSALE

I do appreciate the scientific romanticism of Mister Wells, Doctor, but...

DOCTOR

Herbert may have a few unimportant facts wrong, but his basic supposition is sound enough.[176]

The HG Wells novel Skinsale is thinking of has to be, of course, *The War of the Worlds*, published in 1898. Wells' tale of a hostile Martian force landing on Earth may not have been the very first alien-invasion story, but it established many of the common features of the category – or, one might say, synthesised them. Wells' Martians recapitulate the cephalopodic horrors of earlier 19th-century fiction, while foreshadowing more Lovecraftian abominations:

'There was a mouth under the eyes, the lipless brim of which quivered and panted, and dropped saliva. The whole creature heaved and pulsated convulsively. A lank

---

[176] Episode 3.

tentacular appendage gripped the edge of the cylinder, another swayed in the air'[177]

The aliens harvest human beings for their blood, a detail of obvious contemporary resonance with Bram Stoker's *Dracula* (1897).

The War of the Worlds also channelled the era's vogue for invasion narratives. The fad was sparked by *The Battle of Dorking*, written by British Army General George Tomkyns Chesney in 1871, just after the Prussian army defeated the French at Sedan; Tomkyns imagined the course and aftermath of a German takeover of the British Isles. In its wake came hundreds of similar stories of England overrun by invading forces, sometimes, French, sometimes German. The constant was the implicit (and often explicit) warning against complacency. The Britain that Chesney imagined caught unawares in 1871 ('we had plenty of warnings, if we had only made use of them'[178]) was still being taken by surprise in stories published on the eve of the Great War – as in, for instance, Saki's 1913 exercise in the genre, *When William Came*: 'in less than twenty-four hours those who knew anything knew that the crisis was on us – only their knowledge came too late.'[179]

The famous opening to *The War of the Worlds* put such a warning up front:

> 'No one would have believed in the last years of the nineteenth century that this world was being watched keenly and closely by intelligences greater than man's and

---

[177] Wells, HG, *The War of the Worlds*, p28.

[178] Chesney, George Tomkyns, *The Battle of Dorking*, p17.

[179] Saki, *When William Came*, in *The Novels and Plays of Saki*, p169.

yet as mortal as his own [...] With infinite complacency men went to and fro over this globe about their little affairs, serene in their assurance of their empire over matter.'[180]

Wells might have been simply conforming to invasion-genre expectations; but such over-the-shoulder anxiety also leaked into the real world. Many of the invasion stories were designed as propaganda for increased military spending and planning. The worry reached the halls of government, and Britain began to approach both defence and diplomacy under the assumption of a future conflict with Germany. Preparations for war would eventually become a self-fulfilling prophecy.

The bricolage of tropes Wells assembled provides scaffolding for *Horror of Fang Rock*. It, too, is an invasion story featuring a vampiric, pulsating, tentacular monster. And the characters are most definitely not prepared for the attack, with even the Doctor – the one who does know that the crisis is upon them – unable to forestall the deaths of the others. What is more, there is a sense that the Victorian invasion narratives are very much present in *Fang Rock*'s reality. One would surmise that Reuben is an avid consumer of invasion stories, based on his impressions of the Doctor and Leela:

REUBEN

Foreign, is he?

VINCE

I don't think so. Though 'tis true the young lady speaks a bit

---

[180] Wells, *The War of the Worlds*, p1.

strange. Why?

REUBEN

Could be spies.

VINCE

Spies? What would spies want on Fang Rock?

REUBEN

There's the Frogs, the Russkies, Germans too. Can't trust none of them.

Reuben's reaction to the emergence of a galactic war-front in the Earth's tiny corner of the cosmos is filtered through the kind of nationalistic paranoia aroused by *The Battle of Dorking* and its progeny. The war that such paranoia will spark already lurks at the edges of *Horror of Fang Rock*. The Sontaran-Rutan conflict, a long, exhausting, destructive quagmire, will be recapitulated on a human scale within a few years. The battle at Fang Rock, a grimy, desperate, claustrophobic skirmish, anticipates the futile slaughter of the Great War – the lighthouse's tight stairways resemble nothing so much as trenches. The people are slain, like Wilfred Owen's seed of Europe, one by one, done in by greed, fear, and (on the Rutan's part) a quest for marginal positional gain.

The Lighthouse is explicitly situated in the no-man's-land between history and fiction. Davies acknowledged his source while noting how he took 'considerable liberties' with the Flannan Isles story, even changing 'the name of the lighthouse to Fladda, this being a not unusual name in the Western Isles of Scotland – to avoid offence or distress to any relatives of those concerned in the original incident.'[181] *Horror of Fang Rock* cites the Flannan Isles only at the end, giving retroactive coherence to the similarities of locale and fate. Davies highlights the parallels by denying them at the outset. But both can use the Flannan Isles story to justify their own stranger-than-fiction narratives.

Along the way, *Horror of Fang Rock* even suggests a foundation for literary theory. The peregrinations of Ben's remains demand explanation. Vince sees the corpse in the generator room, then finds it gone; his deduces that Ben has supernaturally got up and walked away. Leela chides Vince for his belief, but then what has happened to the body? When Harker finds the corpse in the sea, and drags it back, Vince doubles down on his assertion. The Doctor's rationalisation is reminiscent of the Flannan Isles: the electric shock that everyone presumed fatal 'simply stunned him, he partly recovered, staggered out onto the rocks, fell into the sea and was drowned.' Vince protests that the body he saw was not breathing. The Doctor closes that plot hole as well:

DOCTOR

Electricity has strange effects, Vince.

VINCE

Oh. Electricity.

But the Doctor is spinning his own story, one he knows to be false. 'Why did you not tell him the truth?' Leela asks. 'Because,' the Doctor replies, 'I don't know what the truth is yet.'[182] Playing for

---

[181] Davies, *The Lighthouse*, p i.
[182] Episode 2.

time, the Doctor inadvertently offers a plausible hypothesis of the cultural origins and persistence of fiction.

4.

Vince latches onto the possibility of Ben's posthumous walk only because Reuben has planted the narrative seed in his imagination. 'If Ben was killed by that damn blasted machine, there'll be anger in his soul,' Reuben warns his young colleague. 'And when they die like that, they'll never rest easy.'[183] Composer Dudley Simpson's cue on the soundtrack at that moment encapsulates much of the musical unease that permeates *Fang Rock*. A bass clarinet creeps furtively up scalar fragments as the harmonic centres shift, not by the more common (and more stabilising) fifths, but by thirds: A, then C-sharp, then E. Against that E, the clarinet climbs to B-flat: a tritone, the most unstable interval in Western tonal music theory.

Simpson's score to *Horror of Fang Rock* works through an entire toolbox of such harmonic instability. One of the predominant sounds is a minor triad, but one divorced from any strong sense of key; instead one hears strings of minor chords, the roots of which are only tentatively related to each other in common tonal practice, if at all. Many harmonies shift between or superimpose major and minor, with both the ambiguity and the half-step sharpness contributing to the tension. And then there is the tritone, outlining or colouring almost every cue in the episode. Even the spaces between Simpson's cues are filled with the sound: the omnipresent foghorn descends B-flat to E – another tritone[184].

---

[183] Episode 1.

[184] That tritone, incidentally, indicates that the Fang Rock foghorn is

133

Nobody on Fang Rock – living or dead – has a chance to rest easy. The music keeps them off balance.

The unquiet dead haunt Davies' lighthouse as well – and the music doesn't just accompany them, it has actually conjured them out of mist and madness. The sorcery, equal parts calculation and intuition, was born of the composer's idiosyncratic relationship with musical modernism.

Peter Maxwell Davies' apprenticeship corresponded with the European-American musical avant-garde's embrace of serialism, an intensely mathematical way of organising music. Serialism evolved out of Arnold Schoenberg's 12-tone technique, developed in the 1920s as a logical framework for the highly chromatic music that came to be called atonality. The concept was simple: rearrange the 12 pitches of the chromatic scale into a row, then use permutations of that row – flipping it, reversing it, transposing it – to generate a work's pitches and harmonies.

After the Second World War, a younger generation of composers applied Schoenberg's methods beyond pitch; rhythm, dynamics, and structure were all yoked to a unifying row. Schoenberg's essentially arithmetic approach was superseded by more

---

cutting-edge technology: specifically, a diaphone foghorn, with motor-compressed air pushed through a sounding chamber open and closed via piston – the second, lower pitch, the diaphone's characteristic 'grunt,' results from the motor stopping the airflow before the piston has completely closed the chamber. The diaphone foghorn was only patented by John Pell Northey in 1903; Trinity House made its first purchase of one of Northey's horns in 1907. See Helbig, William C, *The Diaphone: Its History and Detailed Description*, pp1-2.

complicated mathematics. A group of pitches could yield intervallic and harmonic possibilities under the press of set theory. Rows were organised into matrices of possible permutations and partitions; 12-by-12 grids became a familiar feature of planning and analysing the new music[185].

Davies mastered the techniques. But he also exploited something many post-war composers rejected: the musical past. He referred to and borrowed from older traditions – in particular, Medieval and Renaissance practices. Instead of chromatic rows, Davies constructed matrices from segments of plainchant or other ancient melody. His serialist manipulations echoed similarly intricate processes of Renaissance counterpoint. He developed a skill for musical pastiche and parody, setting his own fiercely stringent style ('My mode of thought is often very complex,' he admitted, early on[186]) in a tense dialectic with sudden irruptions of vernaculars old and new. Reintroducing expressionist unpredictability into serialism's order, Davies became a leading enfant terrible of British music[187].

In the 1970s, Davies went further. He began mapping pitch matrices onto magic squares: equilateral grids filled in with

---

[185] For a concise survey of serialist composition, see Arnold Whittall, *Serialism*.

[186] As quoted on the 26 February 1961 broadcast of the BBC arts programme **Monitor** – in which Davies' early career was contrasted with that of another up-and-coming composer by the name of Dudley Moore.

[187] For a survey and analysis of Davies's music up through the mid-1970s, see Roberts, David, *Techniques of Composition in the Music of Peter Maxwell Davies*.

ascending integers such that each row, column, and full diagonal adds up the same. Magic squares had, over the centuries, acquired mystical connotations, which Davies readily folded into his music. In particular, he utilised magic squares that the 16th-century German alchemist Heinrich Cornelius Agrippa assigned to the sun, the moon, and the five then-known extraterrestrial planets. To generate the materials for his 1975 work *Ave Maris Stella*, for example, Davies refracted a plainchant fragment through Agrippa's nine-by-nine moon magic square; Davies later claimed, citing 'the authority of my instinct, and some listeners' experience of the work,' that *Ave Maris Stella* 'assumed some of the healing properties associated with this square.'[188] Davies amplified vestigial, cabalistic practices lurking in modern music's mathematical rationality.

But one must be careful with the arcane. The magic-square methods governing *The Lighthouse* came with a safety valve, a kill-switch for the numerological engine. 'The forces generated during the composition of *The Lighthouse*,' Davies explained, 'were such that I felt they had to be "spiked" – I therefore introduced specific "wrong" notes into various sequences including magic squares, to neutralise any "Nekuomanteia"'[189].

'Nekuomanteia', consultations with the dead, were a lucrative and often shady business in ancient Greece, so much so that Plato, in his *Laws*, recommended a certain level of regulation. Plato

---

[188] Davies, Peter Maxwell, 'A Composer's Point of View (I): On Music, Mathematics, and Magic Squares', in *Selected Writings*, p217.
[189] Davies, 'A Composer's Point of View (I)'.

classified the unethical behaviour of professional diviners as, essentially, a case of poisoning. In addition to the familiar, biological poisons, 'there is also another kind which persuades the more daring class that they can do injury by sorceries, and incantations, and magic knots, as they are termed, and makes others believe that they above all persons are injured by the powers of the magician,' Plato decreed. 'Now it is not easy to know the nature of all these things; nor if a man do know can he readily persuade others to believe him.'[190]

Ancient literature's most famous example of this communion with ghosts comes in the 11th book of Homer's *Odyssey*. Having tarried for a year on Aeaea, the island home of the goddess and sorceress Circe, Odysseus is finally convinced by his crew to resume their long journey home from war. But first, Circe says, Odysseus must sail to 'Earth's verge' and consult the dead Teiresias, 'that sightless prophet whose integrity of judgement has survived death.' In TE Lawrence's translation:

> 'I drew the keen blade from my hip, to hollow that trench of a cubit square and a cubit deep. About it I poured the drink-offerings to the congregation of the dead, a honey-and-milk draught first, sweet wine next, with water last of all: and I made a heave-offering of our glistening barley; invoking the tenuous dead, in general, for my intention of a heifer-not-in-calf, the best to be found in my manors when I got back to Ithaca; which should be slain to them and burnt there on a pyre fed high with treasure: while for Teiresias apart I vowed an all-black ram, the choicest male out of our

---

[190] Plato, *The Dialogues of Plato*, vol V, p332.

flocks.'[191]

But the first ghost to greet Odysseus after this ritual is that of Elpenor, one of his crew who died on Aeaea after a drunken fall. Elpenor warns Odysseus to return to the island and properly cremate his body, lest the gods use the lapse as an excuse to prolong Odysseus' wandering. On the other hand, when Teiresias does offer his prognosis, it hardly forecasts an expedited arrival:

> 'You come here, renowned Odysseus, in quest of a comfortable way home. I tell you the God will make your way hard.'[192]

In *The Lighthouse*, the dead are awakened not by honey and milk and animal sacrifice, but by song. Davies' keepers are a more volatile group than the Fang Rock crew. Arthur, the veteran, is a Christian zealot, obsessed with rectitude and damnation. Blazes is an aggressive needler, spoiling for a quarrel. Sandy conciliates even as his own temper occasionally flares. After Sandy and Blazes nearly come to blows over a card game, a round of song is suggested: each of the three keepers, buoyed by Davies' skill at pastiche, offers a number to pass the time.

Blazes goes first, with a rollicking music-hall ballad of his own destitute and violent youth – he clubbed an old woman during a botched robbery, then saw his abusive parents blamed and convicted for the crime. Sandy offers a romantic parlour song, Victorian sentimentality that the three men, in a trance, permute and deconstruct into its overtly sexual subtext. Arthur, not

---

[191] Homer, *The Odyssey*, pp148-49, 152.
[192] Homer, *The Odyssey*, p154.

surprisingly, responds with a godly anthem of Old Testament wrath.

As mists descend, ghosts invoked by the songs begin to manifest. Blazes thinks he sees the old lady, covered in gore, and then his parents – his mother driven mad, his father with the marks of hanging on his neck. Sandy is haunted by forbidden loves: his sister first, then a boy, a schoolmate, 'dead and forgotten these twenty odd years.'[193] These are reverse nekuomanteia, the dead summoning the living, beckoning them outside, into the arms of the sea and wind. Arthur proclaims that the Beast is at the door. The men are pinned between the Scylla and Charybdis of Hell and a vengeful God. There is only one solution. The three advance outside to kill the Beast.

As the men go forth and face the Beast's bright white and red eyes, they sing a hymn – marked, in Davies' score, triple-forte and 'bellowing':

> 'From lowest depths of woeful need,
> To God we send our plea,
> To turn his wrath against the Fiend,
> In confidence that we,
> Our vacillating Spirit bared
> In combat face to face
> With Antichrist, will now be spared,
> To wash in divine grace.'[194]

This sermon of pious battle, accompanied by a pungent fog of out-

---

[193] Davies, *The Lighthouse*, pp103-04.
[194] Davies, *The Lighthouse*, pp110-11.

of-tune piano, insistently marches forth. But the howl of sound surrounding it contains a counter-narrative. Flute, clarinet, and violin move together in lockstep, at rhythmic and harmonic variance to the hymn. The three instruments are repeating, note-for-note, the close-harmony chorale announcing the prologue's court of enquiry. The authority of the lighthouse board is descending on the island: 'the three lighthouse-keepers in the doorway become, in a trice, the three officers from the Lighthouse Commission boat.'[195] The blinding glare of the Beast's eyes are the boat's lights. Relief is there, but too late.

'We had to defend ourselves,' sings the first officer, 'God help us.' The story is taking shape. 'They were crazed, run amok,' offers the second officer. 'Explanations will be difficult,' notes the third. 'But who knows what happened?' Only the three officers. So, they devise a plan:

> 'Leave everything in the lighthouse in shipshape order.
> The keepers have gone, disappeared; that's all we know.'[196]

We already know from the prologue that the court of inquiry will accept the story. But the gears of bureaucracy make another turn. The three singers return to the stage as the relief keepers, 'obscure and phantasmal, very suggestive at once of ghosts and automatons.'[197] The music turns spectral, too, as pizzicato strings, guitar, and celesta provide a lattice of harmony: the chords, again, from the prologue's official ritual. The new keepers sing halting, fragmentary echoes of the previous keepers' banal squabbles. The

---

[195] Davies, *The Lighthouse*, p112.
[196] Davies, *The Lighthouse*, pp112-14.
[197] Davies, *The Lighthouse*, p115.

technology of the lighthouse, of both equipment and personnel, has reasserted itself.

The use of role-doubling in *The Lighthouse*, with each of the three singers taking on multiple roles, is at once a practical efficiency, a commentary on the fragility of the characters' psyches, and a portrayal of the dehumanising effect of their work. On the surface, it might be linked to the body-snatching of *Fang Rock* – at a stretch, one might attribute the Rutan's dismissal of humans as 'primitive' to its presumably up-close-and-personal contact with Reuben's hidebound, superstitious self – but its real potency in the opera is how it hints at the conforming pressure of lighthouse duty. The keepers who return at opera's end hover insubstantially between duty and mechanisation. Finally, all that is left is the flashing automated light, as the nine-note apparatus from the beginning returns, repeating over and over again, ever brighter, ever louder.

Gas lighthouses had been automated since the 1890s – a boatman would visit the lighthouse once a week to replenish the gas supply and wind up the clockwork mechanism – but the automatic lamp-changer that enabled the automation of electric lights was only patented in 1928. It wasn't until 1971 that the Flannan Isles lighthouse was automated; one would assume that Fang Rock and Davies' Fladda Isle light went robotic around the same time. But the ending of *The Lighthouse* hints at how events and their retelling might leave long-lingering traces of human drama. If the story is striking enough, it seems, the ghosts take up permanent residence.

5.

According to Davies, *The Lighthouse* was constructed partially based on numerology from the tarot[198]. The 16th card in the Major Arcana of an Italian-suited tarot deck is The Tower, depicting, across many variants, a lighthouse-like stone edifice, aflame, struck by lightning, with two figures plunging from the tower toward the ground. According to French occultist Gérard Encausse, better known as Papus, the Tower 'represents the material fall of Adam,' hence its significations: 'Divine Destruction' and 'The Fall.'[199] AE Waite — co-creator of the Rider-Waite Tarot deck, probably the most common such deck in use — took issue with Papus' biblical interpretation. (Waite's re-designed tarot minimised previous decks' Christian imagery in favour of more generically pagan symbols.) But Waite did agree that the Tower 'signifies the materialisation of the spiritual word.'[200] He assigned similarly dire divinatory meaning to the card:

> 'Misery, distress, indigence, adversity, calamity, disgrace, deception, ruin. It is a card in particular of unforeseen catastrophe.'[201]

Somewhere between Papus and Waite one finds a narrative link between *Fang Rock, The Lighthouse*, and the Flannan Isles mystery: disastrous outbreaks of speculation and lore into material reality. Russian mystic PD Ouspensky allegorised the Tower's intimations

---

[198] Davies, 'The Lighthouse' (programme note), in *Peter Maxwell Davies, Selected Writings*, p146.
[199] Papus, *Le Tarot des Bohémiens*, pp174-75 (translation mine).
[200] Waite, AE, *The Pictorial Key to the Tarot*, p66.
[201] Waite, *The Pictorial Key to the Tarot*, p197.

of the danger of stories by telling a story:

> 'The building of the tower was begun by the disciples of the great Master in order to have a constant reminder of the Master's teaching that the true tower must be built in one's own soul, that in the tower built by hands there can be no mysteries, that no one can ascend to Heaven by treading stone steps.
>
> 'The tower should warn the people **not to believe in it**. It should serve as a reminder of the inner Temple and as a protection against the outer; it should be as a lighthouse, in a dangerous place where men have often been wrecked and where ships should not go.
>
> 'But by and by the disciples forgot the true covenant of the Master and what the tower symbolised, and began to **believe in the tower** of stone, they had built, and to teach others to so believe. They began to say that in this tower there is power, mystery and the spirit of the Master, that the tower itself is holy and that it is built for the coming Master according to His covenant and His will. And so they waited in the tower for the Master.'[202]

This misplaced faith in the Tower marks both *Fang Rock* and *The Lighthouse*. The Doctor thinks he has made the lighthouse a barrier between himself and the threat, but the thick walls instead bring the danger into closer proximity. ('I thought I'd locked the enemy out. Instead, I've locked it in, with us.'[203]) Davies' keepers likewise

---

[202] Ouspensky, PD, *The Symbolism of the Tarot*, pp48-49.
[203] Episode 3.

think the peril is outside. 'God just go on keeping the Beast from the door,' Sandy sings, words that, coming from the shadowy, echoing relief keepers, are the last heard in the opera[204]. But, of course, the beasts have been inside the whole time.

The tarot invades *The Lighthouse* in the form of the Voice of the Cards commenting 'aloft, unseen' as Blazes and Sandy play a game of cribbage.

SANDY

Fifteen, four.

BLAZES

One for his nob.

VOICE OF THE CARDS

As lightning strikes the sea-girt tower, the lamp's snuffed out in a widdershin rout[205].

(In another of the opera's revealing shifts of shape, Arthur and the Voice of the Cards are played by the same singer.) The numbers conjured up by the game turn up again and again in the opera's structure. The Tower, for instance, as the 16th card in the Major Arcana, creates groups and multiples of both 16 and seven (i.e., $1 + 6$) — so the cribbage game is played in seven-beat measures, while, at the opera's climax, the Beast approaches over 16 seven-beat bars. But other such projections happen well below the musical surface; and, as Davies admits, the numbers have been

---

[204] Davies, *The Lighthouse*, pp53, 116.
[205] Davies, *The Lighthouse*, pp59, 60-61.

intuitively altered, or else subjected to the esoteric manipulation of the magic square. The opera's fatalistic course unfolds on a subconscious level.

At the end of their game, Sandy accuses Blazes of cheating ('You fiddled it'[206]). Perhaps the game's web of numerological portent has been shaped by Blazes' fiddling: the cards' eldritch forces have been loosed into the opera's reality by an act of greed and weakness. That creates yet another echo of *Fang Rock*, in which Palmerdale's rapacity and Skinsale's grasping – also very likely the result of a card game – trap and doom the entire complement of Palmerdale's yacht.

One could go on drawing parallels between the two tales: aliens and alienation; disruptive visitors, be they spectral or material; figurative or literal beasts at the door. At a certain point, the similarities stop being coincidence and start hinting at a common mythos surrounding lighthouses in general, and the Flannan Isles light – an acknowledged precursor to both stories – in particular. Perhaps it is time to take a closer look at the Doctor's taste in poetry.

6.

Wilfred Wilson Gibson never saw combat. Gibson volunteered for the British Army four times, and was four times rejected; on his fifth try, he was mustered in as a private, but, by that time, the Great War was lurching its bloody way toward armistice. Gibson's war poetry was a product of his ability to imagine himself into someone else's perception.

---

[206] Davies, *The Lighthouse*, p63.

'I could not understand the sudden quiet –
The sudden darkness – in the crash of fight,
The din and glare of day quenched in a twinkling
In utter starless night.
I lay an age and idly gazed at nothing,
Half-puzzled that I could not lift my head;
And then I knew somehow that I was lying
Among the other dead.'[207]

Gibson may not have made it to the front, but his poems set an example for poets who did. Wilfred Owen, perhaps the most famous of the British war poets, read Gibson's collection *Battle* while being treated for shell-shock; the lean directness and bleak humour left impressions on Owen's own poetry, in which they served a similar purpose: defiantly proclaiming a distinct identity within the war's huge, impersonal machine. Confronted with the enormity of the catastrophe, Gibson used his craft to bring individual experience to the fore. The brevity, the understated language, the unassuming technical precision of meter and rhyme – all tighten and sharpen the focus.

Gibson's ballad of the Flannan Isles feels comparatively slack: garrulous and reiterative instead of concise and straightforward. But, in its own context, the style of 'Flannan Isle' is congruent with its mood. The poem appeared in a 1912 volume, *Fires*, surrounded by other portraits of working-class life. Gibson followed 'Flannan Isle' with 'The Brothers,' a pathos-ridden tale of two feuding, coal-mining siblings who are trapped together after a mine collapse:

---

[207] Gibson, Wilfred Wilson, 'The Quiet', in *Battle*, p39.

'Bob gripped Dick's hand; and then no more was said,
As, slowly, all about them rose
The deadly after-damp; but close
They sat together, hand in hand.
Then their minds wandered; and Dick seemed to stand
And shout till he was hoarse
To speed his winning whippet down the course...
And Robert, with the ball
Secure within his oxter charged ahead
Straight for the goal, and none could hold,
Though many tried a fall.
Then dreaming they were lucky boys in bed,
Once more, and lying snugly by each other:
Dick, with his arms clasped tight about his brother,
Whispered with failing breath
Into the ear of death:
"Come, Robert, cuddle closer, lad, it's cold."'[208]

The comparison with Gibson's portrayal of battlefield death is striking. In the war poems, sudden, arbitrary death creates moments of acute, painful clarity, as if to emphasise the immediacy of the consciousness that is being extinguished. In *Fires*, the effect is of accumulating weight, trying to find a life's meaning and worth in the sheer running tally of memory and day-in, day-out labour. It is near-industrial syntax. In another poem, 'The Machine,' a printer, exhausted by the pre-Christmas rush of producing children's books, feels his identity succumbing to his mechanised routine:

'If only, through his brain, unceasingly,

---

[208] Gibson, Wilfred Wilson, 'The Brothers', in *Fires*, pp52-53.

The wheels would not keep whirring, while the smell –
The oily smell of thick and sticky glaze
Clung to his nostrils, till 'twas hard to tell
If he were really out in the fresh air;
And still before his eyes, the blind, white glare,
And then the colours dancing in his head,
A maddening maze of yellow, blue and red.'[209]

To approach 'Flannan Isle' as a poem about working-class experience is to realise that it is not really about the three disappeared keepers, but rather about the three who discover the disappearance, about men in a dangerous profession coming face-to-face with their own expendability. The heavy tread of the end-stopped lines is equal parts reluctance and dread:

'We landed; and made fast the boat;
And climbed the track in single file,
Each wishing he was safe afloat,
On any sea, however far,
So it be far from Flannan Isle:
And still we seemed to climb, and climb,
As though we'd lost all count of time,
And so must climb for evermore.'[210]

Both the theme and the language here are Sisyphean. And, in Gibson's imagination, the relief crew seems to be looking for gods to blame for their fate. Again, they are put in mind of a purported curse, 'how the rock had been the death / Of many a likely lad':

---

[209] Gibson, Wilfred Wilson, 'The Machine', in *Fires*, p23.
[210] Gibson, Wilfred Wilson, 'Flannan Isle', in *Fires*, p44.

'How six had come to a sudden end,
And three had gone stark mad:
And one whom we'd all known as friend
Had leapt from the lantern one still night,
And fallen dead by the lighthouse wall:
And long we thought
On the three we sought,
And of what might yet befall.'[211]

This macabre history is an invention, but, as we have seen, the idea of a curse fell on fertile ground. Gibson reiterates another fancy, that of the food left uneaten on the table ('We only saw a table, spread / For dinner, meat and cheese and bread'[212]), a detail that appears in none of the official reports; the overturned chair, 'tumbled on the floor,' seems to be Gibson's own embellishment, one that also cemented itself into the popular perception of the story[213]. But again, it is in the accumulation of detail that Gibson's subjects fix the narrative of their own lives, lives otherwise scattered within vast economic, social, or political systems, of which the controls are forever out of their reach.

Of course, as the court of inquiry in *The Lighthouse* shows, details matter in other ways. The bureaucracy might accept their story, but it is because of the discrepancies in their accounts – the chair, the cup, the fauna of Fladda Isle – that the audience's interest and

---

[211] Gibson, 'Flannan Isle', p46.
[212] Gibson, 'Flannan Isle', p45.
[213] Dash, 'The Vanishing Lighthousemen of Eilean Mòr', investigates these and other spurious details in various accounts of the Flannan Isles disappearance.

suspicion are piqued. Is that why the Doctor actually misquotes Gibson? The original poem 'found no trace / Of any kind' of the keepers; but the Doctor's search area is more characteristic:

'Of the three men's fate we found no trace
In any time, in any place,
But a door ajar, and an untouched meal,
And an overtoppled chair'[214]

It is, maybe, a reminder that details don't just provide narrative shape; they provide narrative plausibility.

7.

Throughout *Horror of Fang Rock*, the various denizens of Fang Rock attempt to control their own narratives. Ben perishes early in the story, attempting to maintain his story that electric light is superior to oil, a conviction that has become part of his identity. Palmerdale has outlined his own triumph — he will make it to Southampton, and then to London, and, buoyed by Skinsale's insider tip, will secure his windfall — and the extent to which he will ensure the realisation of his envisioned scenario is profound: neither honour (Skinsale's, or Vince's) nor lives (the crew of his yacht) will deter him. Skinsale's narrative has taken a wrong turn, into possible disgrace; he will destroy the wireless apparatus, the lighthouse's only connection to land and safety, in order to veer that narrative back on to a respectable path. Vince, for his part, sees his plot go awry — into venality and shame, after accepting Palmerdale's bribe — so he burns the money, a ritual sacrifice to the worthiness of his narrative.

---

[214] Gibson, 'Flannan Isle', p46, as (mis)quoted in episode 4.

Adelaide, on the other hand, doesn't so much try to shape her narrative as to retrospectively account for the fact that it has all gone wrong:

ADELAIDE

I told him we shouldn't have come, but he wouldn't listen. He laughed when I said Miss Nethercott had seen tragedy in my stars.

LEELA

In your stars?

ADELAIDE

If only we'd stayed in Deauville. I knew something ghastly would happen. Her predictions are never wrong.

LEELA

I understand. She is your shaman.

ADELAIDE

What? No, Miss Nethercott is an astrologer. The finest. I consult her every month.

Leela's retort – 'I too used to believe in magic, but the Doctor has taught me about science; it is better to believe in science'[215] – underscores the irrationality of Adelaide's narrative strategy. But science, too, is a type of narrative. All of the humans on Fang Rock display this very human behaviour, this need to signify and justify experiences and actions as if they are part of a larger plot, as if

---

[215] Episode 3.

one's life is a novel, or a play – or, at the very least, an episode of a British science-fiction television series.

Interestingly, the nonhuman visitors demonstrate the same compulsion. The Rutan might be on the run from an ignominious defeat, but it will still try to spin it as a story of 'a series of strategic withdrawals to selected strong points.'[216] But the Doctor's narrative strategy is more cagey: in the aftermath, he invokes, by way of Wilson Wilfred Gibson, the Flannan Isles.

It is the same gambit as the officers of the relief ship in *The Lighthouse*. It's not just an alibi; it's a boundary, a narrative box, ready-made for anyone who might confront the mystery. It doesn't matter that the box might be rickety; it doesn't matter that it might be riddled with holes. It fulfils our need for narrative shape. 'All three keepers,' questions one of Davies' conspirators, 'who will believe that?'[217] Everyone will believe it – everyone will believe that the keepers disappeared, and that we will never really know how or why. Only the explanations – every one, by necessity, hypothetical – will vary.

The intrusion of the Flannan Isles into **Doctor Who** – the fact that the Doctor knows Gibson's poem at all – is an especially implicative narrative wrinkle, as it reveals that the Doctor's timeline is one in which both the Flannan Isles and Fang Rock lights exist, in which one mysterious tragedy at a lighthouse follows hard on the heels of another. No wonder the Doctor and Leela don't stick around. Another unexplained lighthouse tragedy? Who will believe that?

---

[216] Episode 4.
[217] Davies, *The Lighthouse*, p113.

The Doctor and Leela slip away before explanation is required. But, just in case, the Doctor rehearses Gibson's ballad. If he needs to give an account, he's got one ready to go. It's all happened before.

EPILOGUE

'May the sons and daughters of affliction be enabled to profit by the bitter lesson with which thou hast seen it meet to visit them. Restore the sick to usefulness, or prepare the dying for judgment and eternity. May the living lay it to heart that they must die, and act as it becometh those who know not how soon they shall be called hence.'

[Rev Alexander Brunton, DD, 'A Prayer for the Use of Those Employed at the Erection of the Bell Rock Light-House' (1807)][218]

One more beacon, one more mystery. Sometime in the late spring or early summer of 1849, Edgar Allan Poe began a story set at a lighthouse, taking the form of old entries – dating from January of 1796 – in the journal of a new lighthouse-keeper taking up his post.

'My spirits are beginning to revive already, at the mere thought of being – for once in my life at least – thoroughly **alone**; for, of course, Neptune, large as he is, is not to be taken into consideration as "society". Would to Heaven I had ever found in "society" one half as much **faith** as in this poor dog...'[219]

The novice keeper, a somewhat high-strung writer, craves solitude, which might be why he is sensitive to any hint of another presence:

---

[218] Quoted in Stevenson, Robert, *An Account of the Bell Rock Light-House: Including the Details of the Erection and Peculiar Structure of That Edifice*, p135.

[219] Poe, Edgar Allan, 'The Light-House', in *Tales and Sketches, Vol. 2: 1843-1849*, p1390. Emphases in the original.

'I could half fancy there was some peculiarity in the echo of these cylindrical walls,' he writes, 'but oh, no! – this is all nonsense.' On his third day of duty, he notes a discrepancy: the floor of the interior seems to sit some 20 feet below sea-level, even at low tide. 'It seems to me that the hollow interior at the bottom should have been filled in with solid masonry,' he opines – 'but what am I thinking about? A structure such as this is safe enough under any circumstances.'[220]

A new light-keeper, his dog, and some odd echoes in the lighthouse walls – and that is as far as Poe went. On October 3, 1849, Poe turned up in Baltimore, incoherent and unkempt, and was taken to a nearby hospital where, four days later, he died. The circumstances and cause of Poe's death have never been adequately explained. Alcoholism, suggested some; suicide by drug overdose, perhaps; or maybe Poe was roped into an election fraud, a victim of 'cooping,' in which bystanders were kidnapped, subdued by drink or drugs, and forced to repeatedly vote for a given candidate. (This could explain why, when he was found in Baltimore, the clothes he was wearing did not seem to be his.) Whatever the scenario, Poe's lighthouse story was left an unfinished fragment.

More than one writer attempted to fill the vacuum of Poe's missing ending. Biographer Kenneth Silverman suggested that the story **was** complete, noting that the date of the final entry in the fictional journal – January 3, 1796 – was the day Poe's mother Eliza arrived in the United States from England; leaving the next day blank, Poe 'vanished himself off the page,' as Silverman put it, closing the

---

[220] Poe, 'The Light-House', pp1391-92.

family's American circle[221]. Author Robert Bloch, at the request of Poe scholar Thomas Mabbott, completed the story, imagining the protagonist combating his loneliness by trying to materialise his thoughts through concentration: first focusing on a rose (which he finds swirling in the waters at the base of the lighthouse) and then on a female companion, who appears at the lighthouse door in the middle of a fierce storm.

> 'Pale lips parted – and I saw the pointed teeth, set in rows like those of a shark. Her eyes, fishlike and staring, swam closer. As I recoiled, her arms came up to cling, and they were cold as the waters beneath, cold as the storm, cold as death.'[222]

Silverman's conjecture has a certain metaphysical wit; Bloch's completion generates an appropriately horrific frisson. But both efforts – all such efforts – are trying to cast a narrative net around something that inevitably slips away. At great cost, Poe produced perhaps the most nagging horror of all: an inconclusive story.

Horror of Fang Rock concludes. It would be strange if it didn't – **Doctor Who** generally wraps up, explains, comes to a conclusion. The Rutan and its mother ship are dispatched. The lighthouse is littered with bodies, but the Earth is saved. The Doctor and Leela return to the TARDIS, off to somewhere else – Titan, maybe[223].

---

[221] Silverman, *Edgar A Poe: Mournful and Never-Ending Remembrance*, p414.
[222] Poe, Edgar Allan, and Robert Bloch, 'The Lighthouse', *Twilight Zone*, August 1982.
[223] *The Invisible Enemy* (1977).

But the Doctor leaves no trace. There is no one else left to tell the tale. All the audience surrogates on Fang Rock are dead; not one remains to reassure us that we all saw what we just saw. It might have been a dream. It might have been shadows in the fog. It might have been a surreal interruption, a temporary deflection of the beacon. Then again – it might have just been echoes in the walls.

BIBLIOGRAPHY

Books

Adams, WH Davenport, *Lighthouses and Lightships: A Descriptive and Historical Account of Their Mode of Construction and Organisation*. London, T Nelson and Sons, 1870.

Allen, Grant, *The British Barbarians*. London, John Lane, 1895.

Allen, Grant, *The Type-Writer Girl*. New York, Street & Smith, 1900.

Bathurst, Bella, *The Lighthouse Stevensons*. 1999. London, Harper Perennial, 2005. ISBN 9780007204434.

Beeton, Isabella, *The Book of Household Management*. London, SO Beeton, 1861.

Bouyer, Frédéric, *La Guyane Française: Notes et Souvenirs d'un Voyage Exécuté en 1862-1863*. Paris, L Hachette et Cie, 1867.

Bradley, Richard, *A Philosophical Account of the Works of Nature*. London, W Mears, 1721.

Chesney, George Tomkyns, *The Battle of Dorking*. 1871. London, Grant Richards, 1914.

Churchill, Winston, *A Roving Commission: My Early Life*. New York, Charles Scribner's Sons, 1930.

Davies, Peter Maxwell, *Selected Writings*. Nicholas Jones, ed, Cambridge University Press, 2018. ISBN 9781107157994.

Davies, Peter Maxwell, *The Lighthouse: Vocal Score*. London, Chester Music, 1982. ISBN 9781847726742.

Davy, Humphry, *Researches, Chemical and Philosophical: Chiefly*

Concerning Nitrous Oxide, or Dephlogisticated Nitrous Air, and Its Respiration. London, J Johnson, 1800.

Davy, Humphry, *The Collected Works of Sir Humphry Davy, vol IV: Elements of Chemical Philosophy*. John Davy, ed, London, Smith, Elder and Co, 1840.

Dicks, Terrance, *Doctor Who and the Horror of Fang Rock*. **The Target Doctor Who Library** #32. London, WH Allen & Co Ltd, 1978. ISBN 9780426200093.

Edwards, George Thornton, *The Youthful Haunts of Longfellow*. Portland ME, Geo T Edwards, 1907.

Ellmann, Richard, *Oscar Wilde*. New York, Alfred A Knopf, 1988. ISBN 9780394554846.

Friedman, John Block, *The Monstrous Races in Medieval Art and Thought*. Syracuse NY, Syracuse University Press, 2000. ISBN 9780815628262.

Fry, Roger, *Vision and Design*. London, Chatto & Windus, 1920.

Gibson, Wilfred Wilson, *Battle*. London, Elkin Mathews, 1915.

Gibson, Wilfred Wilson, *Fires*. 1912. London, Elkin Mathews, 1915.

Goethe, Johann Wolfgang von, *Goethe's Theory of Colours (Farbenlehre)*. Charles Lock Eastlake, trans, London, John Murray, 1840.

Hering, Ewald, *Outlines of a Theory of the Light Sense (Grundzüge der Lehre vom Lichtsinn)*. 1905. Leo M Hurvich and Dorothea Jameson, trans, Cambridge, MA, Harvard University Press, 1964.

Homer, *The Odyssey of Homer*. TE Lawrence, trans, Oxford

University Press, 1991, ISBN 9780195068184.

The International Code of Signals for the Use of All Nations: Prepared Under the Authority of the Board of Trade. London, Sir William Mitchell, 1872.

Jerrome, EG, *Lighthouses, Lightships and Buoys.* Oxford, Basil Blackwell, 1966. ISBN 9780631066705.

Joshi, ST, *HP Lovecraft: The Decline of the West.* Cabin John MD, Wildside Press, 1990. ISBN 9781587150685.

Le Fanu, J Sheridan, *In a Glass Darkly*, vol I. London, R, Bentley & Son, 1872.

Le Gallienne, Richard, *Prose Fancies (Second Series).* London, John Lane, 1896.

Longfellow, Henry Wadsworth, *The Seaside and the Fireside.* Boston, Ticknor, Reed, and Fields, 1850.

Lovecraft, HP, *Miscellaneous Writings.* ST Joshi, ed, Sauk City WI, Arkham House Publishers Inc, 1995. ISBN 9780870541681.

Lovecraft, HP, *Selected Letters: 1925-1929.* August Derleth and Donald Wandrel, eds, Sauk City, Arkham House, 1968. ISBN 9780870540295.

Lovecraft, HP, *Selected Letters: 1929-1931.* August Derleth and Donald Wandrel, eds. Sauk City, Arkham House, 1971. ISBN 9780870540325.

Lovecraft, HP, *Supernatural Horror in Literature.* 1945. New York, Dover Publications, 1973. ISBN 9780486201054.

Machen, Arthur, *Hieroglyphics.* London, Grant Richards, 1902.

Marconi, Degna, *My Father Marconi*. New York, McGraw-Hill Book Co, 1962.

Martin, Martin, *A Description of the Western Islands of Scotland, Circa 1695*. Glasgow, Thomas D. Morison, 1884.

McKee, Christopher, *Sober Men and True: Sailor Lives in the Royal Navy, 1900-1945*. Cambridge MA, Harvard University Press, 2002. ISBN 9780674007369.

Michell, John, *The Flying Saucer Vision: The Holy Grail Restored*. 1967. London: Abacus Books, 1974. ISBN 9780349123196.

Mill, John Stuart, *Principles of Political Economy*. 1848) London, Longmans, Green, Reader & Dyer, 1871.

Minutes of Evidence Taken Before the Royal Commission on Lighthouse Administration. London, Great Britain, House of Commons, 1906.

Ouspensky, PD, *The Symbolism of the Tarot*. AL Pogossky, trans, St. Petersburg, Trood Print and Pub Co, 1913.

Papus (Gérard Encausse), *Le Tarot des Bohémiens*. Paris: Ernest Flammarion, nd.

Plato, *The Dialogues of Plato*, vol V. c400 BCE. Benjamin Jowett, trans, New York, Macmillan and Co, 1892.

Pliny the Elder, *The Natural History of Pliny (Naturalis Historia)*. 79 CE. John Bostock and HT Riley, trans, London, George Bell & Sons, 1893.

Poe, Edgar Allan, *Tales and Sketches,* Vol 2: 1843-1849. Thomas Ollive Mabbott, ed. University of Illinois Press, 2000. ISBN 9780252069239.

Posidippus, *The New Posidippus: a Hellenistic Poetry Book*. Third century BCE. Kathryn Gutzwiller, ed, Oxford University Press, 2005. ISBN 9780199267811.

Price, Martin, *Forms of Life: Character and Moral Imagination in the Novel*. New Haven and London, Yale University Press, 1983. ISBN 9780300028676.

Report of the Commissioners Appointed to Inquire into the Condition and Management of Lights, Buoys, and Beacons. London, George Edward Eyre and William Spottiswoode for Her Majesty's Stationery Office, 1861.

Roberts, David, *Techniques of Composition in the Music of Peter Maxwell Davies*. PhD dissertation, University of Birmingham, 1986.

Rodebaugh, Thomas. *The Face of Evil*. **The Black Archive** #27. Edinburgh, Obverse Books, 2019. ISBN 9781909031791.

Saki (HH Munro), *The Novels and Plays of Saki*. New York, The Viking Press, 1945.

Sederholm, Carl H, and Jeffrey Andrew Weinstock, *The Age of Lovecraft*. Minneapolis, University of Minnesota Press, 2016. ISBN 9780816699254.

> Mayer, Jed, 'Race, Species, and Others: HP Lovecraft and the Animal'.

Seshagiri, Urmila, *Race and the Modernist Imagination*. Ithaca, Cornell University Press, 2010. ISBN 9780801448218.

Silverman, Kenneth, *Edgar A Poe: Mournful and Never-Ending Remembrance*. New York, HarperCollins, 1991. ISBN 9780060923310.

Spengler, Oswald, *The Decline of the West: Form and Actuality* (*Der Untergang des Abendlandes. Gestalt und Wirklichkeit*). 1918. Charles Francis Atkinson, trans, New York, Alfred A Knopf, 1926.

Spengler, Oswald, *The Decline of the West: Perspectives of World-History* (*Der Untergang des Abendlandes. Welthistorische Perspektiven*). 1922. Charles Francis Atkinson, trans, New York, Alfred A Knopf, 1928.

Stephen, Leslie, *An Agnostic's Apology and Other Essays*, 2nd ed. New York, GP Putnam's Sons, 1903.

Stevenson, Robert, *An Account of the Bell Rock Light-House: Including the Details of the Erection and Peculiar Structure of That Edifice*. Edinburgh, Arnold Constable & Co, 1824.

Stevenson, Robert Louis, *Kidnapped*. London: Cassell & Company, Ltd., 1886.

Stevenson, Robert Louis, *Letters and Miscellanies of Robert Louis Stevenson* vol XVIII. Sidney Colvin, ed, New York, Charles Scribner's Sons, 1918.

Stevenson, Robert Louis, *Memories and Portraits*. New York: Charles Scribner's Sons, 1887.

Stevenson, Robert Louis, *The New Lighthouse on the Dhu Heartach Rock, Argyllshire*. Roger G Swearingen, ed, St Helena, The Silverado Museum, 1995.

Stevenson, Robert Louis, *The Works of Robert Louis Stevenson*, Vol 28: Appendix. Edinburgh, T&A Constable, 1898.

Stoker, Bram, *Dracula*. London, Archibald Constable and Co, 1897.

Theroux, Alexander, *The Secondary Colours: Three Essays*. New

York, Henry Holt and Company, 1997. ISBN 9780805053265.

Verne, Jules, *Vingt Mille Lieues sous les Mers*. Paris, J Hetzel et Cie, 1871.

Waite, AE, *The Pictorial Key to the Tarot*. 1911. New York, Cosimo Classics, 2007. ISBN 9781602066786.

Wells, HG, *The War of the Worlds*. London, William Heinemann, 1898.

Whittall, Arnold, *Serialism*. **Cambridge Introductions to Music**. Cambridge University Press, 2008. ISBN 9780521863414.

Wilde, Oscar, *Intentions*. Portland, ME, Thomas B Mosher, 1904.

Williams, Thomas, *Life of Sir James Nicholas Douglass FRS, &c, &c (Formerly Engineer-in-Chief to the Trinity House)*. London, Longmans, Green and Co, 1900.

Woolf, Virginia, *Orlando: A Biography*. 1928. New York, Houghton Mifflin Harcourt, 1973. ISBN 9780156701600.

Woolf, Virginia, *To the Lighthouse*. 1927. New York, Harcourt Brace Jovanovich, 1981. ISBN 9780151907366.

Periodicals

The Chamber of Commerce Journal, October 1900 Supplement.

In-Vision #24, May 1990.

    'Production'.

    Dicks, Terrance, 'The Script Mutations'.

    Freeman, John, 'Light Fantastic'.

'An Act for the Establishment and Support of Lighthouses, Beacons, Buoys, and Public Piers'. US 1 Statute 53–54, 7 August 1789.

'An Act to consolidate and amend the Statute Law of England and Ireland relating to Malicious Injuries to Property'. 24 & 25 Vict c 97, 1861.

'Many Yachts to Go in Commission'. *The American Marine Engineer*, vol X no 6, June 1915.

'Music in Electric Arcs. An English Physicist, with Shunt Circuit and Keyboard, Made Them Play Tunes'. *New York Times*, 28 April 1901.

'Suicide d'un Inventeur'. *La France Libre*, Lyon, 4 November 1898.

'Weekend TV and Radio'. *The Guardian*, 3 September 1977.

Block, Walter, and William Barnett II, 'Coase and Bertrand on Lighthouses'. *Public Choice* vol 140, 2009.

Boston, Richard, 'Enough to drive a man to drink'. *The Observer*, 25 September 1977.

Brown, Paul Tolliver, 'Relativity, Quantum Physics, and Consciousness in Virginia Woolf's *To the Lighthouse*'. *Journal of Modern Literature*, Vol 32, No 3, Spring 2009.

Coase, RH, 'The Lighthouse in Economics'. *Journal of Law and Economics*, Vol 17, No 2, October 1974.

Coase, RH, 'The Problem of Social Cost'. *Journal of Law and Economics*, vol 3, no 1, October 1960.

Dash, Mike, 'The Vanishing Lighthousemen of Eilean Mòr'. *Fortean Studies*, vol 4, 1998.

Dash, Mike, 'True Strange Stories?' *Fortean Times* #352, April 2017.

Fallon, Ernest, 'The Strange Log of the Seven Hunters'. *True Strange Stories*, vol 1, no 6, August 1929.

Gilbert, W Stephen, 'The Week in View'. *The Observer*, 28 August 1977.

Marconi, Guglielmo, 'Wireless Telegraphy'. *The Electrician* #1086, 10 March 1899.

Miéville, China, 'MR James and the Quantum Vampire'. *Collapse IV*, May 2008.

Mildren, Richard, Aaron McKay, Ondrej Kitzler, Robert Williams, David Spence and David Coutts, 'Diamond Enables Combination of Non-Collinear Kilowatt Beams'. *SPIE Newsroom*, 29 September 2016. (DOI: 10.1117/2.1201608.006667, accessed December 19, 2018.)

Pixley, Andrew, 'You Ain't Seen Nothing Yet'. *Doctor Who Magazine* Special Edition #8, cover date September 2004.

Poe, Edgar Allan, and Robert Bloch, 'The Lighthouse'. *Twilight Zone*, August 1982.

Raman, CV, 'A New Radiation'. *Indian Journal of Physics*, vol 2, 1927.

Schultz, E, 'The Samoan Version of the Story of Apakura'. *The Journal of the Polynesian Society*, vol XVIII no 70, June 1909.

Solomon, Richard L, and John D Corbit, 'An Opponent-Process Theory of Motivation: I. Temporal Dynamics of Affect'. *Psychological Review* vol 81, no 2, 1 March 1974.

Stevenson, Robert Louis, 'The Education of an Engineer'. *Scribner's Magazine*, vol IV no 5, November 1888.

Stockton, Sharon, 'Public Space and Private Time: Perspective in *To the Lighthouse* and in Einstein's Special Theory'. *Essays in Arts and Sciences* vol XXVII, October 1998.

Thompson, Silvanus P, 'The Arc Light' (I). *Journal of the Society of Arts* no 2240 vol 43, 25 October 1895.

Tyndall, John, 'Goethe's Farbenlehre (Theory of Colours)'. *Popular Science Monthly*, vol XVII, no 19, July 1880.

West, John B, 'Humphry Davy, Nitrous Oxide, the Pneumatic Institution, and the Royal Institution'. *American Journal of Physiology: Lung Cellular and Molecular Physiology*, vol 307 no 9, November 2014.

Television

Doctor Who. BBC, 1963-.

Doctor Who: Thirty Years in the TARDIS. BBC, 1993.

Monitor. BBC, 1958-65.

Web

'Max Headroom WTTW Pirating Incident – 11/22/87 Subtitled'. https://www.youtube.com/watch?v=tWdgAMYjYSs. Accessed 28 December 2018.

'Statistics.' *Doctor Who Guide*. https://guide.doctorwhonews.net/info.php. Accessed 7 January 2019.

Bonhams, 'Books, Maps, Manuscripts, and Historical Photographs, Including the Property of the Late Michael Silverman'. 22 November 2011, Lot 200.

http://www.bonhams.com/auctions/18992/lot/200/. Accessed 7 January 2019.

Briggs-Ritchie, Joe, 'The Ballad of Fang Rock'. *The Doctor Who Ratings Guide*, 8 May 2010. http://www.pagefillers.com/dwrg/horr.htm#20. Accessed 18 February 2019.

Crab, Simon, 'The "Singing Arc": William Duddell, UK, 1899'. *120 Years of Electronic Music.* http://120years.net/the-singing-arcwilliam-duddeluk1899/. Accessed 19 December 2018.

Davies, Daniel, 'Shine Your Light on Me…' *Economics and Similar, for the Sleep-Deprived*, December 23, 2002. http://blog.danieldavies.com/2002/12/shine-your-light-on-me.html. Accessed 10 December 2018.

Helbig, Lieutenant William C, USCG, *The Diaphone: Its History and Detailed Description*. Groton, MA, Coast Guard Training Station, Aids to Navigation School. https://www.gllka.com/1953-uscg-diaphone.pdf. Accessed 25 February 2019.

Independent Institute, 'The Lighthouse Logo'. http://www.independent.org/aboutus/lighthouse.asp. Accessed 10 December 2018.

Knittel, Chris, 'The Mystery of the Creepiest Television Hack.' *Motherboard*, 25 November 2013. https://motherboard.vice.com/en_us/article/pgay3n/headroom-hacker. Accessed 28 December 2018.

Lovecraft, HP, *The HP Lovecraft Archive*. Loucks, Donovan K, ed. http://www.hplovecraft.com/.

'The Call of Cthulhu'.
http://www.hplovecraft.com/writings/texts/fiction/cc.aspx.
Accessed 13 December 2018.

'The Colour Out of Space'.
http://www.hplovecraft.com/writings/texts/fiction/cs.aspx.
Accessed 2 January 2019.

'The Dream-Quest of Unknown Kadath.'
http://www.hplovecraft.com/writings/texts/fiction/dq.aspx.
Accessed 20 February 2019.

'The Horror at Red Hook'.
http://www.hplovecraft.com/writings/texts/fiction/hrh.aspx
. Accessed 13 December 2018.

'The White Ship'.
http://www.hplovecraft.com/writings/texts/fiction/ws.aspx.
Accessed 6 December 2018.

Woolf, Virginia, and Vanessa Bell, '"Hyde Park Gate News", a
magazine by Virginia Woolf and Vanessa Bell'. British Library.
https://www.bl.uk/collection-items/hyde-park-gate-news-a -
magazine-by-virginia-woolf-and-vanessa-bell. Accessed 17 October
2018.

BIOGRAPHY

Matthew Guerrieri is a musician and author who regularly writes about music for the *Boston Globe* and *NewMusicBox*; his articles have appeared in *Vanity Fair*, *The American Scholar*, *Playbill*, and *Musical America*. He is the author of *The First Four Notes: Beethoven's Fifth and the Human Imagination* (2012), named a best book of the year by *Los Angeles* magazine, *Time*, and *The New Yorker*. He is currently working on a global history of music in the 1950s.

Coming Soon

#34: Battlefield by Philip Purser-Hallard

#35: Timelash by Phil Pascoe

#36: Listen by Dewi Small

#37: Kerblam! by Naomi Jacobs and Thomas Rodebaugh

#38: The Underwater Menace by James Cooray Smith

#39: The Sound of Drums / Last of the Time Lords by James Mortimer

#40: The Silurians by Robert Smith?

#41: Vengeance on Varos by Jonathan Dennis

#42: The Rings of Akhaten by William Shaw

#43: The Robots of Death by Fiona Moore

#44: The Pandorica Opens / The Big Bang by Philip Bates

#45: The Unquiet Dead by Erin Horáková

#46: The Awakening by David Powell

#47: The Stones of Blood by Katrin Thier

#48: The Tenth Planet by Michael Seely

#49: Arachnids in the UK by Samuel Maleski

#50: The Day of the Doctor by Alasdair Stuart

#50A: The Night of the Doctor by James Cooray Smith